(

# TEN WORDS OF FREEDOM

# TEN WORDS
# OF FREEDOM

## AN INTRODUCTION TO THE FAITH OF ISRAEL

By JAY G. WILLIAMS

FORTRESS PRESS

Philadelphia

*Library of Congress Catalog Card Number 73-139344*

ISBN 0–8006–0131–9

14941170     Printed in the United States of America     1-30

**TO  HERMINE**

## CONTENTS

# INTRODUCTION

Since the time of Moses numerous and varied works have been written about the Ten Commandments. There are midrashim and haggadoth, commentaries and homilies, histories and novels. There are even, may mankind be forgiven, a few movie scripts. Why then write—or read—another book concerning this subject? Are there not already more than enough volumes in print about the Decalogue, its historical or moral significance, to satisfy the interested reader?

The answer to these questions must be metaphorical. In the life of each man there are certain events which serve as "turning points." Some of these events occur as a result of careful premeditation; others break into life without conscious thought or effort. Some are immediately recognized as significant; others only reveal their importance with the passing of time. These events are, as it were, the keys to the mystery of a man's existence. If he is reflective at all, he will return to them in memory again and again to unlock their meaning, to reassess them, and to stand in awe before the singularity of these moments which have shaped his own uniqueness.

Not only individuals but also communities and civilizations have memories. Just as the individual finds his uniqueness in the private memories which are his, so we, as a people, discover our special place within the order of things by returning to those corporate memories which are ours. We are who we are because of those meaningful events which have drawn us together as a people. We may repudiate these memories, as an old man repudiates the follies of his youth, but we cannot forget them without destroying our own self-identity.

One such event which has marked out our particular historical path is the exodus. Although only a few of us are blood descendants of the men who stood before the mountain of Sinai, all who have lived in Christendom have been "grafted into" this memory. Through the advent of Jesus of Nazareth the memories of ancient Israel became the memories of the Christian church and then of Western society in general. Israel's flight from Egypt became a turning point, Israel's covenant a matter of self-identification for all of us. Nor does the widespread rejection of these memories in our age negate this fact. Our culture may be post-Christian, but it is post-*Christian*. If we who live among the ruins of a devastated Christendom are to understand our situation aright, we must be keenly aware of the memories which constitute us and must return to them in all seriousness so that both present and past may be illuminated.

Today, we stand at the threshold of a new age, the age, as Harvey Cox has said, of the "Secular City."[1] Indeed, if Cox is correct, we have already crossed the frontier and have begun to settle in the city called technopolis. The folkways of our "town culture" are being cast aside as we become more and more pragmatic, urban, and secular. Is this the turning point of turning points? Now that we see our immediate destiny before us, must we cast aside the hopes and dreams of our forefathers as illusions? Were their turning points really only unfortunate excursions down blind alleys or is there a hidden line of destiny which runs from those earlier turning points, through ours, to some distant, or perhaps not so distant *telos?*

1. Harvey Cox, *The Secular City: Secularization and Urbanization in Theological Perspective* (New York: Macmillan Co., 1965), passim.

Cox claims that there is such a line. He argues that the events of the exodus and Easter have prepared the way for the Secular City and offer us many clues as to how we may approach this new world of mobility, anonimity, and pragmatism in which we find ourselves. He believes, indeed, that the Secular City is a partial fulfillment of the hopes of Israel. There is no need for us to review and criticize here his specific arguments for this position. What is important is that we ourselves return to the exodus, not just to play games with Semitic cognates nor to concoct fanciful theories about what "really happened," but to examine this remembrance of things past in the light of our own unique situation.

We must recognize, moreover, that as the memories of Israel become ours once more they will inevitably be transformed. Memories are not just static facts; they are like precious jewels which reflect ever-new radiance as the light of the centuries changes. The ancient priests of Israel found in the exodus implications for their lives of which Moses undoubtedly never dreamed. The prophets, in their turn, discovered new dimensions of the covenant neglected by the priests. And Jesus, who ushered in a decisively new age, unfolded to his disciples hidden meanings in Scripture to which previous generations had apparently been blind. If we are to follow in the footsteps of the prophets and apostles, we too must rediscover and transform the memories of Israel according to our own experience.

We must be aware that this is a difficult and perilous task. It is one thing to view our memories from a new perspective and to find new illumination on the basis of the past; it is another to read into the past dishonest rationalizations or to deal insincerely with the intentions and faith of those who have gone before us. He who contemplates the memory of his people must do so with great humility lest he destroy, through flippancy or arrogance, his own self-identity.

Our reading of the Bible is analogous to old men trying to understand the attitudes and actions of youth. Try as we may, the values and aspirations of the younger generation escape us—as irresponsible, idealistic, or irrelevant. We do not understand or appreciate their customs or their language. The wise adult, however, seeks neither to deride nor explain away the actions of young men. Instead, he seeks to view them with compassionate imagination, hoping thereby to comprehend both their vitalities and their apathies. Ultimately, their mystery may escape him, just as his existence is an enigma to them; yet youth and old age are bound together, if not by perfect comprehension and agreement, by the fact that young men will one day be old and old men, though they can scarcely imagine it, were at one time young.

In this volume we shall proceed word by word and line by line through the Decalogue of Exodus 20, trying to ferret out the meaning of each commandment. Whenever relevant, philological and historical information will be introduced to clarify the significance of the text. We shall also savor the richness of the Hebraic motifs and metaphors implicit in the text and seek to understand them within the context of the rest of Scripture. To understand in depth the concepts and motifs used in this text is to understand the very heart of biblical theology. Therefore, it is hoped that this work will serve not only as an interpretation of the Ten Commandments themselves but also as an introduction to the faith of Israel as a whole.

If one wishes to understand the Bible, it is never enough, however, just to analyze biblical vocabulary and thought-forms. We are modern men remembering our own past, and therefore we must put to our past the questions which disturb us today. We must both hear the questions which the Bible raises for us and ask of the Bible those questions prompted by modern historiography, natural science, and philosophy. In a word, we must enter into genuine dialogue with the text. Only in this way will our past and our present illumine each other.

Our task then has three interrelated phases. We must ask: What does the Decalogue mean in and of itself? How is it related to the basic themes of Scripture? How is it related to us? In each chapter we will deal with these three questions as the various themes of faith present themselves. Needless to say, I make no claim to having raised all of the relevant questions or having given fully adequate answers. The more I study the Ten Commandments the more I discover what an inexhaustible source they are for understanding God, man, and the universe. Perhaps the most that I can hope to have done in this work is to have proved once more the truth of Philip Melanchthon's remarks: "The contemplation of the Decalogue is altogether useful and salutary, for it contains such wealth and loftiness of doctrine that it can never be fully conceived and exhausted."[2]

I would like to express my thanks to the Ford Foundation for a grant which greatly facilitated the preparation of the manuscript for this book, to the late R. Glynne Lloyd for his helpful advice, and to Mrs. Mary Mosley for her careful clerical assistance.

2. Quoted by Solomon Goldman, *The Ten Commandments,* ed. Maurice Samuel (Chicago: University of Chicago Press, 1956), p. 84.

# PART I:

# THE PROLOGUE

"And God spoke all these words, saying . . ."

## Chapter 1

# HISTORY AND THE
# WORD OF GOD

"And," the first word of the introduction to the Decalogue of Exodus 20, is perhaps theologically insignificant and could be passed over cursorily by the exegete. Still, it does indicate that the Decalogue is directly related to the historical events which precede it and therefore can be taken as an opportunity to discuss the relation between history and revelation. "And" is a sign, albeit a subtle one, that the words known as the Ten Commandments were derived, not through mystical or rationalistic speculation, but through a listening to the historical process.

This notion, that biblical revelation is historical revelation, has been greatly emphasized by many biblical theologians in recent years. At the same time, the discovery of this basic biblical motif has led to some perplexing problems. While theologians have stressed the historicity of God's word, historians have come to some rather negative conclusions concerning what we can really know historically about many of the key events of Israel's history. For instance, of the exodus event Martin Noth writes:

There can be no doubt, however, that this was a real event; we can discern to some extent the conditions and circumstances which led to it and can fit it into a historical situation of which we have quite reasonable knowledge. The incident itself, which the Israelites experienced as an unexpected and mighty act of deliverance of their God, remains veiled from our sight.[1]

The question which this modern historical judgment raises is this: Does the fact that we can, historically speaking, know little or nothing about what actually happened to Israel in her flight from Egypt and in her sojourn at Sinai mean that it is no longer possible for modern men to "hear" the living God of Israel speak? How can modern men receive a revelation through events which are no longer experienced or known by them? These are difficult questions which must not receive perfunctory answers. If we are to speak of the God who promulgated the Decalogue as the God who brought Israel out of Egypt, we must ask in what sense, if any, this event can be regarded as historical.

Perhaps the best way to begin to resolve this difficulty is to compare and contrast modern and biblical historiography. In so doing it will be necessary to caricature both somewhat, for there are many differences among various modern historians and among the various authors of the Bible. Basically, however, the distinctions between modern and biblical historiography are reasonably clear.

## OBJECTIVE HISTORY AND THE PAST

"History," as it is used today in common parlance, has two rather distinct meanings. On the one hand, it can refer to the creative work of a historian who writes a history of this or that. Thus John Bright has written *A History of Israel*. On the other hand, "history" often refers to the past events themselves. History, in this sense, is understood as being like a great bottomless pit which contains all of the significant and insignificant events which have ever occurred. The task of the historian is to find evidence of these events and write about them in an objective fashion.

1. Martin Noth, *The History of Israel*, revised translation by P. R. Ackroyd (New York: Harper and Brothers, 1960), p. 117.

This double meaning of the term leads, unfortunately, to a subtle, but important linguistic confusion. For instance, when we ask whether an event is historical or not, we usually do not mean to ask whether it was recorded but whether it "really happened." Some recorded events (for example, the story of Adam) may not, in this sense, be historical at all. At the same time, when we speak of a prehistorical event we mean that it may have happened, but was not immediately recorded because it occurred before mankind had begun to create written records. Thus we speak, in a very strange way, of the "prehistorical history" of our planet.

Not only is this double meaning of the word "history" confusing, it is based upon a philosophically untenable belief that there are such things as objective events which exist apart from human perception of them. An event, as it is normally defined, means "an occurrence, a happening, something which presents itself to us." The last phrase is particularly important. An event is such only when it presents itself *to someone.* Without a sentient observer there can be no event. It is true, of course, that we can describe unseen events like the classic tree falling in the forest without anyone around, but we can only describe them as they would have been seen by us had we been there. Therefore, there is no such thing as a purely "objective" event. An event, by definition, demands a subjective observer.

Furthermore, and this is an equally important point, different observers may well see the "same" event in quite different ways. Take for example the "event" of a cow swishing its tail. This event doubtless would be seen quite differently by the cow, the flies on the cow's back, and the farmer milking the cow. In fact, the sentence "The cow swished its tail" is a purely human description. We cannot describe how the other sentient participants viewed the event at all.

Not only does man's view of an event differ from that of other sentient creatures. Different men may see the "same" event quite differently. Suppose, for instance, that four people attend a showing of Cecil B. DeMille's *Ten Commandments.* The first, an expert color photographer, will notice various photographic techniques completely missed by the others. The second, a biblical scholar, will doubtless feel his blood rising as he sees the original story distorted. The third, a man whose fiancée is among the cast of thousands, will pay attention to her part in the story. The fourth, a two-year-old baby, will experience something—but who can describe what he sees? In other words, although we may say uncritically that they all see the same movie, each will see something quite different.

Because we live in a culture where most men share the same general world view, we are apt to conclude that there is one "objective" view of an event. The truth of the matter is, however, that people from different cultures and different times differ decisively concerning their vision of events. The fact is that although most men have the same sensory apparatus, what they sense is profoundly shaped by what they expect to perceive, by what their particular world view tells them is real.

This is not to say that a person's or a culture's world view can never change. There are times when events prompt men to reconsider their own basic presuppositions. If this were not so, mankind would still be living in the Paleolithic Age. A world view is born out of the impact of the "givenness" of events upon the life of a people. But an event is never a virgin birth. The language, the mythology, and the traditions of a people dramatically shape the impact which such givenness has. An event has such givenness as its father, but the womb which gives it birth is the world view of the people.

All of this means, of course, that when a modern historian describes the events of the ancient past, what he really describes is the product of the givenness of history combined with his own world view. This world view determines the events which he chooses as important to describe, the explanations which he offers for these events, and, in fact, the way he pictures them as having occurred. Because ours is a scientific age, modern historiography is inevitably scientific. That is, the explicit and implicit ground rules

6

which nearly all historians use today are established by the so-called scientific viewpoint. I say "so-called" because many scientists today have now gone beyond the rather mechanical Newtonianism of the past and are exploring speculative ideas which may greatly reshape the common world view of the future. At this point in human history, however, most historians accept a rather Newtonian standard for understanding the past. What are some of the assumptions which these historians make?

First of all, although these assumptions are not usually clearly articulated, the modern historian makes some presuppositions about the nature of time. Man is conceived as living on a quantifiable temporal continuum which proceeds ever onward from past to future. Once an event has occurred it is immutably fixed forever. We can redress wrongs done in the past, but we can never change them. The future, on the other hand, has not yet "happened" and hence is unknowable. To be sure, the historian, like anyone else, can make calculated guesses about what will happen, but because of either the lack of complete knowledge (if one is a determinist) or the freedom of man (if one is a voluntarist) no one can know for sure what the future holds in store. This means that claims made by others about the future must be regarded with suspicion.

Between the immutable past and the unknowable future lies the present, an infinitely thin dividing line. Somehow we live in the present; yet by the time we know the present, it is already past.[2] Time, as experienced, is the present in which we live, but that present is not a quantifiable continuum but "living duration." The

2. E. A. Burtt writes, "Consequently time seems to us nothing but a measurable continuum, the present moment alone exists, and that moment itself is no temporal quantity but merely a dividing line between the infinite stretch of a vanished past and the equally infinite expanse of the untrodden future. . . . We are forced to view the movement of time as passing *from* the past into the future, the present being merely that moving limit between the two. Time as something *lived* we have banished from our metaphysics, hence it constitutes for modern philosophy an unsolved problem." Edwin Arthur Burtt, *The Metaphysical Foundations of Modern Physical Science* (Garden City, N.Y.: Doubleday Anchor Books, 1954), p. 95. See also Karl Heim, *Christian Faith and Natural Science* (New York: Harper and Brothers, 1957), p. 57 ff.

past lives within us as memory; the future shapes us with its hopes and promises and threats. Because of the impact of Newtonianism, however, we have come to think of, and even "experience," time as a measurable continuum governed by the clock.

Strangely enough, while the man on the street still thinks in this "Newtonian" way, natural scientists now conceive of time quite differently. Not that they have returned to time as experienced. Rather they have developed theories concerning the relativity of time which are, for the layman, counterintuitive and which seem to turn our whole world view topsy-turvy. While the biblical historian confidently assumes that the past is past and the future is future, the physicist speculates about sending up a rocket so fast that it will come back yesterday.[3] We must grant, of course, that such speculation is just that. As far as we know there is a speed limit in the universe, the speed of light, which would make such a venture impossible. Nevertheless, it is "conceivable," given the view of time prevailing among scientists in this post-Einsteinian era. Time is regarded, not as an absolute continuum, but as a relative relation between masses in motion. Surely the biblical theologian must be very careful not to use such speculation in order to "prove," for instance, the visions of the future attested to in the Bible. Nevertheless, the theory of relativity should at least shake the supreme confidence of those who say that knowledge of the future is impossible and therefore delete all purported visions as "later additions."

The second assumption which the biblical historian takes from science concerns "natural law." The world, it is presupposed, operates according to certain laws which have been in effect from the "beginning." Therefore, a report of a natural law being "broken" must be regarded with great suspicion.[4] If, for instance, it is

---

3. Lincoln Barnett, *The Universe and Dr. Einstein* (New York: New American Library of World Literature, 1957), p. 46 ff. See also Sir James Jeans, *Physics and Philosophy* (New York: Macmillan Co., 1943), p. 63 ff.

4. This seems to be a basic position underlying Bultmann's argument for demythologizing. He writes, "It makes no difference in principle whether the earth rotates round the sun or the sun rotates around the earth, but

claimed that Jesus walked upon water, the story, as a factual account, must be criticized, for according to "natural law," men cannot walk upon water without artificial aid. Hence, the exegete must either give a naturalistic explanation (it was an optical illusion) or a symbolic interpretation (this myth reveals that Jesus is triumphant over the floods of disaster which confront man) or must treat the story as a result of superstition or wanton lying.

These are attractive alternatives to the dogmatic acceptance of every detail of Scripture urged by some theologians of the past. Surely faith should not be equated with simpleminded credulity. Nevertheless, it must be pointed out that most sophisticated scientists no longer speak about discovering natural laws. The task of the scientist today is most frequently not conceived as the discovery of certain immutable laws but only as the describing of those consistencies which are perceived. The modern scientist observes and experiments, noting the consistent operation of the phenomena under consideration. Because his observations must, by their very nature, be limited, he cannot reject arbitrarily a report of some event which doesn't seem to fit into his description of the consistencies of the cosmos. Rather he must examine the validity of the report and, if necessary, revise his own description accordingly. If it is impossible to examine the report's accuracy, then he must, as a scientist, reserve judgment. "Impossible" is a word which the empirical scientist ought not to use about events in this world. "Improbable" is the strongest word in his vocabulary.

Another means by which historians evaluate accounts of the strange and wonderful in Scripture is through an appeal to the findings of the anthropologists. For instance, in order to cast doubts upon such an "event" as the Virgin Birth, historians point

it does make a decisive difference that modern man understands the motion of the universe as a motion which obeys a cosmic law, a law of nature which human reason can discover. Therefore, modern man acknowledges as reality only such phenomena or events as are comprehensible within the framework of the rational order of the universe." Rudolf Bultmann, *Jesus Christ and Mythology* (New York: Charles Scribner's Sons, 1958), p. 37. Used by permission.

to parallel accounts of similar births witnessed to by other religious traditions. Presumably the fact that many ancient religions taught a belief in one or more virgin births proves that the authors of Scripture simply adopted familiar religious symbolism of the time to communicate certain ideas. Again, such a line of argumentation is sometimes convincing, particularly for those who, because of faith in natural science, find it difficult to believe that a human conception could occur without benefit of human sperm. Nevertheless, from a purely logical point of view the existence of reports of other virgin births says nothing about the validity of the biblical report. Just as the fact that many reports of flying saucers are hoaxes proves nothing about the validity of other reports, so the fallaciousness of some accounts of some "wonders" says nothing about the rest. I do not mean to argue here that modern man must accept all the "miracle" stories found in Scripture if he is to be "religious." Faith must not be equated with gullibility. I only wish to argue that modern man should not be gullible when confronted by counterarguments offered in the name of science. Oftentimes belief in these arguments entails just as much credulity as belief in the biblical account.

Because of modern technological achievements there is a great temptation for us to think that our way of "seeing" is far superior to that of men of previous generations. Such scientific and technological advances, however, should not obscure the fact that in developing our own world view we have also lost much. Ancient men could see many things to which we are blind. In fact, there are very few modern men who could exist under the conditions in which ancient bedouin tribesmen thrived. The modern "scientific" world view works fairly well in our generation, but it would have been quite useless for the people of Israel wandering in the wilderness. The idea of Moses setting up a laboratory in the wilderness to perform experiments is too ludicrous to consider.

Moreover, it is by no means clear that the chief end of man is merely either to go farther faster or to survive under the harsh conditions imposed by the wilderness. In order to decide which world view "works best" we must first decide what the end of man is or should be. Modern science and technology have done much to make our lives more comfortable and efficient, but they have not been so effective in promoting a sense of brotherhood among men or in providing any ultimate meaning for human existence. In fact, the sense of alienation and despair which pervades modern culture seems to be due, at least in part, to the objectivizing and pragmatic spirit of modern scientific thinking.

As we read the Hebrew Scriptures we cannot avoid using our own scientific knowledge to understand the text, for we must begin where we are. At the same time, Israel's *sui generis* perceptions and understanding must not be looked upon with condescension. Before we attempt to "correct" her vision of life and reality, we must first listen to her and learn as best we can how she perceived and understood the events of her life. If we are to comprehend the Bible at all, we must, through imagination, try to understand as the biblical writers understood. Only then can any decision be reached as to the validity of the biblical message.

## BIBLICAL HISTORIOGRAPHY

When we turn from modern historiography to the Bible, we immediately enter another, quite different, world. Indeed, if one takes the modern conception of history as normative, the Bible does not appear to be history as all. Not that the events referred to in Scripture did not "happen." Archaeologists and historians have proved quite conclusively that from a modern historical point of view many of them did.[5] Nevertheless, Israel understood and described these events in ways which differ quite radically from the way a modern historian would understand them.

The first major difference between modern and biblical historiography involves the understanding of time itself. Modern men conceive of events as occurring within a chronological time con-

5. William Foxwell Albright, *From the Stone Age to Christianity* (Garden City, N.Y.: Doubleday Anchor Books, 1957), pp. 200–272.

tinuum which is totally quantifiable. Time is divided into seconds, minutes, hours, days, months, years, etc. and these time units are ticked off with precise regularity. All events are fitted into this continuum and therefore can be dated exactly and absolutely.

The ancient Semite also knew the reality of years, months, and days (although classical Hebrew has no words to express the concepts of hour, minute, and second), but he did not think of these realities as purely quantifiable and objective. Rather a year was conceived as an enduring reality which meets man in the autumnal rains and then lives out its life until, after a summer of scorching heat, it dies. Man meets the month in the new moon which waxes and then in waning expires. The day confronts man in the setting of the sun, in the radiant fingers of the dawn, and in the searing heat of midday. No two days are alike. Each has its own special character which distinguishes it from the others.

It is noteworthy that the Hebrew word for time ('ēt) is derived from a root meaning "to occur or to meet." Man does not just live in time; he meets a time which is always related to this or that specific occurrence or recurrence. Perhaps, then, it is better to speak not of "time" but of "times." Everything—the moon, the nesting heron, the rain, the sun—has its time, but there is no one universal time matrix in which all things live and move which is known to man. From a human point of view, time is relative, not absolute.

It is also significant that the only Hebrew word which might be translated "history" is the word *toldot* which means primarily "generations." History, for the Israelite, was not measured by the ticking of some cosmic clock but by the duration of generations. Every generation knows a time, dwells in a time, encompasses a time. This time is the lived-out duration which begins when the first vague memories are formed and lasts until the eyelids of death are closed. It is a time shared by a community of persons, a time with a particular tempo, rhythm, and style. Abraham had a time, a time of promise, movement, and conflict. When Isaac was born, Abraham's time did not end, but endured until it had run its course. Isaac's time, however, began exhibiting, as it continued, its own peculiar characteristics.

History, then, cannot be conceived as a simple progression of one irreversible moment after another. For the Bible different generations, and hence different times, may exist concomitantly. History is not so much like a monophonic chant as like a very complex polyphonic motet in which new "themes" are regularly introduced and developed. These themes conflict with, answer, and influence one another as they run their courses.

Closely related to "generational time" is what might be called "royal time." Again, this time should not be confused with or reduced to purely quantified chronological time. A "royal time" is an era dominated and shaped by the style and power of a particular king. For instance, the time of David was an era of unique tempo and rhythm which depended, at least in part, upon David himself. No other time has been quite like it, for David made it unique. Because such "royal times" normally do not overlap, they are useful in fixing chronological dates. Nevertheless, from the point of view of the biblical writers, "royal time" is not to be reduced to quantified time; quantified time is subordinate to "royal time." "In the fifth year of King Jehoiakim" and "in 604 B.C." may appear to the modern historian to be equivalent, but for the Israelite they would not have been. The former refers to a particular stage in the development of the style and tempo fostered by a ruthless despot. The latter refers to the overarching rhythm of history set by the King of Kings, Jesus.

Biblical man, then, as he lives and meets the recurring realities of his world, experiences many different times. The question remains: Is there any overarching time in terms of which all of these "met" times can be understood? Man's situation is a little like that of an observer of a performance by a modern musical ensemble in which several conductors conduct, with seeming independence, various suborchestras and choruses. From the point of view of the observer it may appear that each conducted time exists independently of all the rest. What he cannot see is that there is one hidden conductor and one time according to which all the other times are to conform. The fact that what is played is music and not just noise may cause him to postulate a hidden conductor, but until the final coda is played, the real time may remain hidden.

So it is, for the Bible, in the world. God, too, has a time, but his time is hidden from man. Unfortunately, Christian theologians have, for centuries, labored under the influence of Greek metaphysical thought and hence have often conceived of the biblical God as infinite, unchangeable, and timeless. Recent research has made quite plain, however, that the Hebrew word, *'olam*, which is usually translated "Eternity," has no implications of timelessness. *'Olam* is hidden time, transcendent time; yet it is time.

A second difference between biblical and modern historiography relates to the respective attitudes toward the consistent operation of the "natural" world. Modern historians, under the influence of the natural sciences, are usually quite critical of any report of phenomena which seems to "fly in the face" of discovered natural laws. Stories of fire descending from heaven, or miraculous cures, or floating axe heads are consigned, for the sake of consistency, to the realm of legend.

The writers of the Bible, in general, are not so fastidious in this regard. Not that they do not believe that the world operates in a consistent fashion. On the contrary, because of their belief in God's consistency, they often are as bewildered by the wonders they report as a modern man might be. Furthermore, on the whole, the Bible is quite soberly realistic when compared to the myths and legends of other ancient peoples. Nevertheless, biblical writers do not discard the reports of strange phenomena simply because they are strange; they include them because they are remembered as having happened.

The Bible accepts throughout the consistent operation of the universe, but attributes the reality of this consistency not to any abstract natural law but to God himself. The so-called miracles, though seeming to be examples of God's inconsistency on a physical level, are taken to be signs of his ultimate consistency in regard to his attitude toward man. For the Israelite, God's failure to bring Israel out of Egypt would have been an inconsistency on his part of the first magnitude. Therefore, when Israel exults in the fact that God has led her out with signs and wonders, she affirms not the inconsistency but the consistency of God.

A third difference between modern and biblical historiography involves the way in which the events themselves are described. Modern historiography tends to be generalized and abstract. What are sometimes called concrete facts are actually abstractions from experience. For instance, a sentence such as "World War II lasted from 1939–45" involves considerable abstraction from concrete experience. In contrast, biblical historiography seems much closer to life itself. Although Israel sometimes generalizes about her experience—as the sentence, "I am the Lord your God who brought you out of the land of Egypt," clearly indicates—the reader of the Bible often feels a direct relation to the event which much modern historiography fails to provide.

At the same time biblical historiography also involves a kind of abstraction from experience which must not be overlooked. For instance, in the book of Exodus little attention is paid to the visual sense. We are told virtually nothing about the physical characteristics of Moses or of the beauties of the Pharaoh's palace. Even the location and topography of Mount Sinai are left unspecified. Instead, careful attention is paid to what is said. The book of Exodus is primarily a transcription of conversations between Moses and God, the people, Aaron, and the Pharaoh. Reading this book is like listening in on a party line to someone else's conversation. One can understand the essential plot, but the names, dates, and locations are often left to the imagination.

Furthermore, it is clear that not all events experienced are mentioned in the text. Rather, certain events are chosen to be recorded while a singularly large number are simply omitted. The principle of selection is made clear in the accounts of the dreams and visions of various characters, for in them the destiny of the

15

people is often described. These accounts not only have the function of providing a perspective to the narrative so that the reader may understand the significance of the events he is "witnessing"; they also provide a basis for determining which events are to be described in the text. Thus, although the Bible provides us with an account of events as they might have been "heard" by a contemporary, it also gives us the perspective of "eternity" according to which these events may be understood.

Such an approach to history has disadvantages which modern readers are not slow in recognizing. We would like to know more precisely when, where, and how such events took place. We want names, dates, and locations more carefully specified. Furthermore, even the nonscholarly reader may suspect that the "perspective of eternity" has not only influenced the selection of material to be included in the text but has also caused the history to be considerably altered in order that it might conform to the general theological thesis which undergirds the narrative. Such questioning is, of course, legitimate. Although it appears that in general the Bible is historically accurate, there are also indications that the story has been modified considerably in some places to express better the theological predilections of the "authors." Nevertheless, biblical historiography has certain values to which we should not be blind. A comparison of the following accounts—one modern and one ancient—of the same event makes the nature and significance of the biblical approach quite clear.

> Already by 616 B.C. the battles were chiefly taking place simply around the central land of Assyria and Mesopotamia which adjoined it on the west; the other parts of the empire that had known such greatness until recently no longer played any part at all. These battles led to the royal Assyrian city of Nineveh falling into the joint hands of the Babylonians, Medes, and Umman-manda in 612.[6]

> Woe to the bloody city,
> all full of lies and booty—

6. Noth, *The History of Israel,* pp. 270–71.

no end to the plunder!
The crack of the whip, and the rumble of wheel,
        galloping horse and bounding chariot!
Horsemen charging,
        flashing sword and glittering spear,
        hosts of slain,
            heaps of corpses,
        dead bodies without end—
            they stumble over the bodies!
And all for the countless harlotries
            of the harlot,
        graceful and of deadly charms,
    who betrays nations with her harlotries,
        and peoples with her charms.
Behold, I am against you,
        says the Lord of hosts,
        and will lift up your skirts over your face;
    and I will let nations look on your nakedness
        and kingdoms on your shame.
I will throw filth at you
        and treat you with contempt,
        and make you a gazingstock.
And all who look on you will shrink
        from you and say,
Wasted is Nineveh; who will bemoan her?
        whence shall I seek comforters for her?
                                (Nahum 3:1–7).

The first quotation is historically accurate, succinct, and to the point; yet it is removed intellectually and emotionally from the event. It does not describe what concretely happened but only speaks in the most general way about this occurrence. The second quotation, on the other hand, brings us right into the heart of fallen Nineveh. In a few brief lines the reader himself experiences the event in all its confusion, bloodiness, and shame. The date, the names of the victors, the historical background are left unspecified; yet the essence of the event in all its fullness is communicated.

Perhaps the most important distinction between modern and Israelite historiography is to be found in a comparison of these two passages. The modern historian begins with the assumption that he is dealing with events only as they happened to someone else. He tries, therefore, to regard them from a neutral, objective standpoint. The writers of Scripture, however, take quite the opposite view. For them, events must be described as they occurred. Furthermore, because these are Israel's experiences and because the writers are sons of Israel, these events are thought of as occurring to them.

### MEMORY, THE CORPORATE PERSONALITY, AND HISTORIOGRAPHY

Modern, particularly Anglo-American, men regard society from the perspective of the reality of the individual. That is to say, families, tribes, and nations are conceived of primarily as collections of individual persons who happen to have joined together in a community. Even the family is regarded by many as a society formed for the convenience of the individual rather than vice versa.

In order to understand the Bible the reader must recognize that the ancient Israelite took quite the opposite point of view. For him the people of Israel as a whole was the primary human reality; individuals were but cells in Israel's body and had to be understood in this social context. Israel was thought of as a living reality, a person who was born, bred, and now lives in the present generation as a corporate reality. Just as in the human body where individual cells continually expire but the body lives on, Israel persists despite the passing of the generations.

This concept of what has been called the "corporate personality" of Israel[7] is particularly important for an understanding of Israel's historiography. Just as all nonneural human cells, according to biologists, are completely replaced in a few brief months while the individual remains the same self-conscious person, so Israel changes and yet remains the same. How? What unites the individual as a person? Here we arrive at a mystery. The cells change and yet the personal identity remains—because of the continuity of memory. When a person loses his memory, he also loses his

7. H. Wheeler Robinson, *Corporate Personality in Ancient Israel,* Facet Books, Biblical Series 11 (Philadelphia: Fortress Press, 1964).

sense of self-identity. So it is with Israel. One generation follows another, but Israel lives on as a self-conscious "person" because she remembers her past.

Central to Israel's remembering are, of course, the Law and the Prophets. Here Israel's memories are preserved for posterity; here is the very core of her personal identity. Recent research into the means by which such memories were preserved in ancient times has shown that the term "memory" is far more than just a figure of speech.[8] Long before the Torah became a series of five written scrolls it was preserved, in embryonic form at least, in the memory of the people by a process known as "oral transmission." In brief, the whole process by which the Torah took shape may be described in this manner: Soon after an event of significance took place, the poets and storytellers set about to commemorate it through the composition of poems and sagas. Their song grew slowly as it was chanted before the people. What was considered by the community to be accurate and properly expressive was accepted. What was not was rejected and forgotten. As new events took place, these too were commemorated and the song-tale grew. Sometimes years passed before anything new was added, but gradually, the saga as we now have it took shape as the living memory of the people.

During the course of years the tale not only grew; it was also refined and embellished. Names of places were brought up to date to make the narrative more understandable to the contemporary hearer. Other traditions, perhaps sometimes even written documents, were welded or absorbed into it in order to express new meanings found in the event. In the light of later experience, whole sections might be added, subtracted, or recast. Thus, the memory lived on, though often in a dramatically altered way.

Finally, the tradition, after years of growth and development, was committed to writing. Just when this took place is not certain. I myself, believe that the postexilic date suggested by Eduard Nielsen is far too late.[9] After all, writing had been known and prac-

8. Albright, *From the Stone Age to Christianity*, p. 64 ff.
9. Eduard Nielsen, *Oral Tradition* (Naperville, Ill.: Alec R. Allenson, 1955), p. 39 ff.

ticed in Canaan for centuries. It seems incredible that Israel would have waited so long to commit her memories to writing.[10] At the same time, it must be remembered that even after the Torah had been set down in written form, the written tradition still depended upon the oral tradition rather than vice versa. In fact, it may be said that the written Torah was used primarily as a help in remembering. Only the consonants were written; no attempt to separate words was made. Hence only someone who was already acquainted with the text could read it without some pondering. Perhaps it is enough to say that the Torah was not fixed in writing until sometime after the major portion of the tradition had been fused together into one narrative. Anything which was added to the text after that time was undoubtedly minimal—a scribal gloss here or an emendation there. Any major changes which took place probably began in the oral tradition first and were only added to the written tradition after they had been firmly established orally.

It may seem incredible to modern men that the whole of the Torah could have been committed to memory by anyone, for most of us have difficulty memorizing even a few lines of poetry. This, undoubtedly, is because we modern men no longer cultivate our memories but depend upon books instead. In ancient times—and even in many cultures in the twentieth century—such was not and is not the case. Albright writes:

> Even today Moslem boys learn the Quran by heart and use the printed text only to correct mistakes. The same is said to be true of Hindu students of the Vedas to this day and the practice of committing the Chinese classics to memory only began to disappear in the past generation. Down to the World War Jewish students of the Bible and Talmud in Eastern Europe often memorized large parts—in extreme cases even the entire Bible or (mirabile dictu!) Talmud.[11]

10. Against this position it could be argued with some cogency that the Talmud remained in only oral form for centuries, even though the transmitters themselves could read and write with ease. On the other hand, both the Gospels and the Koran, though undoubtedly originating in oral tradition, were put in writing relatively early.

11. Albright, *From the Stone Age to Christianity,* pp. 64–65.

There is no doubt that the men of Israel remembered their traditions in the same way. In fact, it would be extraordinary if such were not so. To think of the traditions of Israel as being written first by authors who composed the stories *de novo* is to misunderstand the whole nature of religious tradition.

Today we might also question the accuracy of such a means of transmission. Would not this method of learning and transmitting the Torah by rote allow all kinds of discrepancies and variations to creep into the text? If the memory of Israel rests upon oral tradition, does it not rest upon a very insecure foundation? Of course, there is no foolproof means of transmitting anything from one generation to another. On the whole, however, it can be said that oral transmission was usually a far more accurate way of passing on a tradition than was the written text. A scribe might miscopy a line or willfully introduce a change in the text without being discovered. If the text were not memorized, readers could be easily fooled. In oral transmission, however, such a change would be readily caught by the alert and well-trained listener. Since mistakes of memory were seriously frowned upon, the chanter sought for accuracy.

This general thesis is borne out by the Bible itself. Much to the surprise of many would-be skeptics, modern archaeologists have discovered that the Bible contains very ancient memories which are accurate in minute detail. The sagas of Abraham, for instance, reflect with more than casual accuracy the geography and population of Canaan during the patriarchal period. Again, Albright writes:

> The picture of movements in the hill country of Palestine, of seasonal migration between the Negeb and central Palestine, of easy travel to Mesopotamia and Egypt is, accordingly, so perfectly in accord with conditions in the Middle Bronze Age that historical skepticism is quite unwarranted. When we add the fact that our present knowledge of social institutions and customs in another part of northern Mesopotamia in the fifteenth century (Nuzi) has brilliantly illuminated many details in the patriarchal

stories which do not fit into the post-Mosaic tradition at all, our case for the substantial historicity of the tradition of the Patriarchs is clinched.[12]

Since the Torah then is the memory of Israel and bears some analogous relation to the memory of the individual it may be fruitful to examine the memory of the individual for further clues about how the Torah took shape. Perhaps the most important feature of memory is that in memory no past event is simply "dead." Although an event may have occurred, in every age the memory of that event, in the light of more recent events, may assume new significance. The rememberer may or may not be conscious of his change in attitude; but the attitudes will change and hence the memories will be subtly altered.

This is precisely what happened to Israel's memories. When Israel returned in memory to the covenant at Sinai she did not only ask, "What did God say to us then?" She also asked, "What does that event mean to us now?" In one age, Israel heard a cultic word from God, in another a word of judgment, in still another a word of social legislation. All these words she included in the text.

For the historian who looks at the past as dead and unchangeable, this is a very confusing process. He wants to discover what "actually happened" and cast off all the rest as "later additions." This is, however, to misunderstand the whole process of memory. For the Israelite, hearing the word which God spoke at Sinai afresh was not reading into the event something which was not originally there. It was rather hearing more clearly what God said but what men had not really understood.

It is also noteworthy that our most important memories—the ones which shape our personality most deeply—are our earliest ones. By the time a child is five his personality is already well formed. At the same time, these early memories, though vastly important, are also often quite confused. We may remember certain details very well, but cannot remember when or where the

12. William Foxwell Albright, *The Biblical Period from Abraham to Ezra* (New York: Harper and Row, 1963), pp. 4–5.

event took place. The chronology of our early life may be thoroughly jumbled in our memories. Did Grandpa die before or after I went to New York City by airplane? Such questions are often difficult to answer without consulting an "outside source."

The same is true with the memories of Israel. The books of Genesis and Exodus are full of flashes of memory which bear many marks of authenticity but which are, nonetheless, quite confusedly put together. Modern archaeologists have confirmed that many of the customs mentioned in Genesis, for instance, reflect very accurately the times of the patriarchs. Nevertheless, there hangs over the book of Genesis a cloud of confusion. Sometimes the most amazingly inconsistent statements are placed side by side. This, of course, is quite understandable according to our analogy. Israel remembers her childhood as we do, in brilliant flashes and vague recollections. Her "elders" always seem very old; yet her own actions seem very youthful. Everything is confusion, wonderment, and activity. The very vagueness of many passages, though difficult to interpret, attests to the antiquity of the text.

Another point which should be made about memory is that it is shaped by the way in which it is articulated. If, for instance, we were called upon regularly to witness in a meeting to our religious experiences, our witness would soon take on a particular form. When we tell tales of our past to our children our stories are shaped by that context. We omit certain details; we embellish others. This is also true of Israel's memory. Undoubtedly her tale is shaped in part by the mnemonic techniques used by the chanters. The use of this chant in the liturgy of worship and praise also doubtless had its effects. Many of the sudden breaks in the text, doublets, and curious fusions may be explainable by reference to the cultic use to which the text was put. Form critics have done much to illumine this whole area of research, but their work has been severely impeded by the fact that we know very little about the early use of the Torah in the cult. Nevertheless, it seems reasonably clear that a more thorough understanding of Israel's cultic practices would greatly illumine the development and organization of the text. It is to be hoped that in the future new discoveries will be made which will shed light upon this aspect of biblical studies.

Throughout this discussion of the formation of the traditions of Israel nothing has been said thus far about the standard theory about the composition of the Torah, that is, the "documentary hypothesis." This has been the case because this writer believes it is no longer possible to write with scholarly assurance about the documentary sources of the Pentateuch.

A full discussion of documentary and source criticism lies beyond the scope of this work. Perhaps all that ought to be said here is that although it is quite clear that there are several "strata" of tradition within the Torah, the distinguishing of these strata is so complex and unproductive that it ought, perhaps, to be foregone for the present. In any event, what we shall concentrate upon in this work is the completed Torah, the memory of Israel as it finally crystallized, rather than upon the elements which constitute it. This approach has been chosen, not only because the separation of sources is difficult but because in disentangling the various strands of tradition it is all too easy to overlook the unity and the argument of the book as it stands.

## CONCLUSION

We began this discussion of Israel's view of history with a question to which we must now return: If the God of Israel is known through history, how can modern men believe in him if that history is now objectively unavailable? How can we hear God speak in the exodus if, as an objective historian like Martin Noth says, we can know little or nothing about that event historically? I have attempted to show that modern biblical theology has arrived at this seemingly insurmountable impasse because we have made a false distinction between historical events in and of themselves and man's apprehension of them.

Let us define history, then, as a record of man's experience and understanding of events. Not that experience and understanding can really be separated. Because man is a self-transcendent creature, he is not just a passive recipient of simple perceptions. Rather man's experience itself is shaped decisively by his world view, interests, and inclinations. There is, of course, a "givenness" in experience which cannot be denied. No one can "make up" history. Indeed, the givenness of unique events often has an impact upon a person's world view and interests which may dramatically alter the individual's and the society's outlook. History is born from the dialogue between this givenness and man's preconceptions.

The history of Israel as it is recorded in the Torah is particularly complex because this dialogue is not limited to one individual's or one generation's dialogue with certain given events. The story of the exodus, for instance, is really told from many points of view all at once. The impact which the event had upon the original Israelites fleeing from Egypt is embellished and transformed by its impact upon succeeding generations. What we hear in the book of Exodus is not a solo voice proclaiming the importance of this event for him but a whole chorus of voices from different generations.

The modern historian, in his attempt to discover what "really happened," tries to circumvent this sometimes confusing chorus by relying primarily, if not exclusively, upon archaeological and other extrabiblical evidence. What he does, however, is simply to add another voice, albeit an "objective" one, to the chorus. Modern histories of Israel are the records of the dialogues between the "givens" of history and the scientific world view of modern man. Since scientific objectivity precludes the possibility of hearing God speak, it is no wonder that the word of God is absent in them.

If one wishes to hear God's word in the events of Israel's history, one must listen to the whole chorus of voices which are heard in Scripture. This word is to be found neither in simply the givenness of events nor in the world view of the observers but in the interaction, i.e. in the events themselves. Thus, although we may not be able to reconstruct what happened "objectively" and therefore cannot know the event in a positivistic sense, the word spoken through the event to generations of Israelites is still available. Archaeology may help us to learn about biblical times, but if we wish to hear the word which God spoke to Israel in the exodus we must listen to Scripture, for the Bible contains the events as they were heard by generations of Israelites. Before we can discuss the meaning of the word witnessed to and expressed in the book of Exodus, however, we must turn to another question: What does the Bible mean by the word "God"? Only when we have answered that question can we return to the question, what did God say?

# Chapter 2

# "GOD"

It is no longer a secret to anyone that the word "God," which has served so many generations of philosophers and theologians in Western culture as a central presupposition for systematic thought, is today under fire. Philosophers, whose intellectual ancestors once used the concept of God as a cornerstone for their thinking, now question whether the word has any meaning at all. The fashion of the day is neither atheism nor even agnosticism but what might be called "I-don't-know-what-you-mean-ism." This attitude is not so much a defiant rebellion against the claims of biblical faith as it is a simple inability to see any relevance or meaning in those claims at all. As Karl Heim has so convincingly pointed out, the modern secularist just doesn't see a need to postulate or believe in any supernatural being or cosmic person.[1]

In one sense, of course, there is nothing new about this attitude. There have been many philosophers in the past who have questioned the meaning of the word God. What is rather unique is that this attitude is now reflected by so many "laymen" within our society. Today, it is the man on the street who, when he hears the word God, wrinkles his brow and says, "I'm sorry, but I do not understand what you mean." With his world view so shaped

1. Karl Heim, *Christian Faith and Natural Science* (New York: Harper and Brothers, 1957), pp. 11–24.

by a popularized version of modern science he sees no particular reason to accept the traditional theological answers to questions he no longer asks.

Even the theologians who are professionally committed to the study of *theos* and thus have the most to lose if the word turns out to be a nonsense syllable have begun to reflect the spirit of the times. William Hamilton and Thomas Altizer proclaim that God quite certainly is dead;[2] John A. T. Robinson declares that at the very least the concept of God needs complete redefinition;[3] Harvey Cox suggests that a moratorium be called and that the word God not be used until the air has cleared a little.[4] The interpreter of the Bible, therefore, can no longer simply pass over the word God as though it were intelligible to all.

Defining the word God as it is used in the Bible, however, is not an easy assignment, for the Bible itself never seems to offer any definitions or even univocal descriptions of the deity. Metaphor is piled upon metaphor; anthropomorphisms and anthropopathisms abound, but nowhere is there a passage which declares: this is what "God," in nonmetaphorical terms, means. Tillich may speak of God as Being-itself or as the ground of Being,[5] but the Bible *seems* to avoid any such attempt to find an "anchor" for its metaphors. Instead, Scripture consistently confines itself to describing what this undefined God has done in the life of Israel. Indeed, one might well draw the conclusion that the God of Israel can only be described in this way. The actions, but not the essence, of God can be known.

Such a refusal to say anything about God in nonmetaphorical language raises some difficult questions of interpretation. The

2. Thomas J. J. Altizer and William Hamilton, *Radical Theology and the Death of God* (Indianapolis: The Bobbs-Merrill Co., 1966), passim.

3. John A. T. Robinson, *Honest To God* (Philadelphia: Westminster Press, 1963), ch. 2.

4. Harvey Cox, *The Secular City: Secularization and Urbanization in Theological Perspective* (New York: Macmillan Co., 1965) p. 266.

5. Paul Tillich, *Systematic Theology*, vol. 1 (Chicago: University of Chicago Press, 1951), p. 235 ff. Tillich alternates, in a rather confusing way, between a conception of God as Being-itself and a conception of him as the ground of Being.

Bible, for instance, uses the metaphor of fatherhood; God is called the Father of Israel. In saying this the text seems to imply that God's relation to his firstborn son is something like a human father's relation to his son. But how is the fatherhood of God like the fatherhood of man? Is not some anchor for the metaphor needed in order to make it meaningful? Tillich tries to answer this question by saying, in effect, that human fatherhood is to divine fatherhood as finite being is to the ground of Being. Since Tillich believes that the word Being can be spoken univocally,[6] he thinks that he has a cognitive basis for understanding all biblical metaphors.

Unfortunately, the anchor which he chooses seems to many to be thoroughly nonbiblical. The concept of Being is Greek, not Hebraic, and hence is rejected by many biblical theologians as misleading. This may be so. Nevertheless, the exegete must not fail to see that the problem with which Tillich deals is a real one. Therefore, he cannot return to the language of pure metaphor without searching for a more biblical anchor according to which such symbolic language can be understood.

A clue to the solution of this difficult problem is to be found in the word used most commonly in the Old Testament to refer to God, that is, *'Elohim*. Although this word is often translated simply "God," our English word scarcely begins to capture the connotations of the Hebrew. In the first place, this word, which is etymologically related to the word *'El*, the name of a Canaanite god, can be translated simply "Powers." The God who speaks to Israel at Sinai is "the Powers." Second, it should also be noted that when used with a plural verb the word can also be rendered "angels" or "gods." In fact, in the first commandment, *'Elohim* is used to refer both to the "other gods" which Israel is no longer to "have" and to the *'Elohim* of Israel, Yahweh. Since Scripture itself makes this connection between the God of Israel and the gods of the pagans, we may do well to begin by examining the nature of the gods whom Israel is called to foreswear.

6. Ibid., p. 238.

## THE GODS

If one can speak of a "natural religion" of mankind at all, one might say that it was—and perhaps is—polytheism.[7] At least, polytheism seems to be the natural development and fulfillment of more "primitive" types of religion found among preurban peoples. While monotheism, at least in its biblical form, came into being through what seems to be an inexplicable leap, polytheism seems to have developed rather naturally among men without any cataclysmic revolution.

Needless to say, not all forms of polytheism were exactly alike. Not only did the names of the gods and goddesses change from country to country, but their characteristic "essence" varied too. Herodotus' attempt to understand the Egyptian gods as the Greek deities with different names was, even for many ancient men, misguided and laughable.[8] Nevertheless, polytheism is basically the same wherever it is found.

Because of centuries of Christian polemic and the so-called scientific temper of our times, most people today look back upon the polytheisms of ancient man with religious abhorrence, scientific disdain or perhaps, if tolerance is the watchword, with historical forbearance. Christianity has long condemned and scoffed at polytheism as primitive superstition and to this extent, at least, most modern thinkers would agree. Even most atheists believe, though rather inconsistently, I think, that monotheism represents a higher stage in the development of religion than polytheism. Polytheism is associated with primitive barbarity and prelogical, antiscientific thinking and thus is dismissed without a hearing.

Before the religion of polytheism is discarded so quickly, however, it may be well to examine more carefully what the polytheist was trying to express. There was a time when intelligent, well-educated, and thoughtful men—artists, poets, philosophers, and

7. David Hume offered some cogent arguments for this position in his *Natural History of Religion*, ed. H. E. Root (Stanford, Calif.: Stanford University Press, 1957).
8. Sir Alan Gardiner, *The Land of the Pharaohs* (New York: Oxford University Press, 1966), p. 4.

statesmen—were polytheists. Neither Aeschylus nor Virgil was a fool. How could these men have been so easily deluded by the religion of their day that they did not see the weaknesses apparent to us? Who were the gods they worshipped and why did they believe in them?

One common answer to this question offered by modern men runs something like this: Ancient man was surrounded by many seemingly inexplicable mysteries which puzzled him. Where does the sun go when evening comes? Why does summer inevitably follow spring and spring follow winter? Why do sudden storms with their strange thunder and lightning arise? For these and many other questions ancient men sought answers. They had, however, no adequate methodology for finding truly scientific solutions to their problems and therefore constructed myths to explain what they could not understand. When asked about the rising and setting sun the Egyptian would tell stories about Rē and his daily journey through the sky to the region under the earth. When confronted by a fierce storm, the Babylonians would speak of Enlil, the god of the storm, who brings such catastrophes to the wide plains of Mesopotamia. When questioned about the thunder and lightning, the Greek parent would tell his child stories of Zeus, the king of the gods, who rules through the power of the thunder bolt. Scientific discoveries, of course, have shown these myths to be only pseudoscientific explanations. Hence, it is impossible any longer to accept these ancient stories of the gods as true. Myth has now been replaced by a much more accurate form of knowledge, namely, science.[9]

If ancient myths were meant to function as scientific explanations, this "modern" attitude toward the myths of polytheism would be quite justified. Insofar as a myth purports to be a "scientific explanation" it is subject to scientific criticism. There are good reasons, however, for suspecting that such was not usually

9. For a reasonably clear statement of this position see Hans Reichenbach, *The Rise of Scientific Philosophy* (Berkeley, Calif.: University of California Press, 1963), pp. 5–9.

the purpose behind myth making. Admittedly, men of antiquity did sometimes try to explain the causes of mysterious phenomena through etiological myths. And there were some critics of religion, such as Lucretius,[10] who interpreted all myths in this way. It is by no means clear, however, that all or even most ancient myths were meant to be etiological, at least in a pseudoscientific sense. The fact is that men of antiquity knew much about the "natural" causes of physical phenomena. For instance, though the Egyptians told and retold the stories of Osirus, they knew that the waters of the Nile brought fertility to their land. They devised irrigation systems and learned to predict the time and extent of flooding quite accurately. The growth of such science and technology did not mean the death of mythology, however, for a belief in Osirus and irrigation existed comfortably side by side. This would seem to indicate that the stories of Osirus, Isis, and Horus were meant to be something other than scientific explanations. This conclusion is supported by the fact that ancient polytheism was finally conquered, not by science and technology but by Judeo-Christian monotheism.

If ancient men did not use myths to explain and describe the efficient causes of physical phenomena, what purpose did they serve? As indicated above, the Hebrew word, 'Elohim, which means literally "Powers," offers a clue. If this word is taken as paradigmatic, a god should be thought of as a power, that is, as "that which or one who exercizes authority or influence over human life."[11] The polytheistic mythologizer, then, simply sought to describe the variety of powers which affect man. He was not just a superstitious man purveying silly stories about imagined deities. Rather he was seeking to describe as concretely and as carefully as possible the powers which actually exerted influence over the lives of human beings.

10. Lucretius, *The Nature of the Universe,* trans. Ronald Latham (Baltimore: Penguin Books, 1965), pp. 29–31.
11. *The American College Dictionary,* ed. Clarence L. Barnhart (New York: Harper and Brothers, 1948), p. 950.

This is, perhaps, the most characteristic feature of the mythologizer. He does not try to speculate about what the world is like apart from man. He develops no abstract notions about being and becoming or about atoms and the void, but instead, through the medium of poetry, tries to express the impact which the various powers of the universe make upon man, how they confront man, and how they are related one to another. The scientist may examine the meteorological causes of the sudden storm. The philosopher may search for principles for understanding change. But the mythologizer simply describes how the storm confronts man concretely and directly. Admittedly, the "Powers" which the mythologizer describes always remain hidden from man; we simply cannot know what these "Powers" are like in and of themselves. From that point of view, they transcend human experience. Nevertheless, even the most hardened skeptic who denies the possibility of any knowledge of the world and the powers inherent in things,[12] must admit that certain "Powers" do affect his life. Nothing is more indubitable than the force with which political power or sexuality or commerce influences a man's existence.

The mythologist who describes these "Powers" soon learns that if he is to be honest he must describe them in certain ways. In the first place, he must recognize that because he seeks to describe "the Powers" as they directly affect men he must speak of them as "Thous" rather than as "Its." The weatherman who describes a hurricane from the secure perspective of his office may speak in terms of quantifiable meteorological forces. The mythologizer, however, stands with the man in the midst of the storm who shakes an angry fist and curses the "Power" which has destroyed his home and family. The weatherman as weatherman must say "It"; the suffering human overwhelmed by disaster is compelled to say "Thou."

12. John Locke denied that we can know the powers inherent in things and, of course, in one sense he was correct. We cannot know the power of gravity itself, but only those effects which it produces. Nevertheless, when an apple strikes us on the head or when "Cupid's arrow strikes," we cannot deny that some power has affected us.

One major objection to this use of "anthropomorphic" language is that it is an attempt to make nonhuman realities in man's image. Human beings, it is argued, are properly addressed as persons, but trees, stones, and sociological forces are not. Martin Buber has reminded us, however, that this criticism misses the point of such a use of language. When one says "Thou" one does not speak of some psychical properties of the object addressed but rather expresses an attitude of the speaker as he is confronted.[13] As a matter of fact, from an "objective" point of view, it is no more legitimate to say "Thou" to a man than to a stone. When considered purely as an object of scientific investigation, man is known simply as a thing among other things. For a scientist as scientist, man is an "It" to be examined, quantified, and explained. Conversely, when a tree confronts man with beauty and grace, the only proper response may be to say "Thou."

Many modern men will still not be satisfied by this defense of polytheism. The man in the midst of the storm may, it might be argued, speak anthropomorphically, but we know objectively that the storm is merely a quantifiable physical force. The tree may elicit a "Thou" from man, but in itself is still just a tree and no more. Although poetry is the natural response of man in certain situations, it is not as accurate as natural science. Poetry describes men's feelings; science describes the world as it is.

Such an attitude is so widely accepted in the twentieth century that it is virtually impossible to argue against it without developing a whole new metaphysics and world view. Perhaps, however, the basic point to be made is this: neither poetry nor science can bring us knowledge of the world as it exists in and of itself. Both attempt to describe man's experience of the world from a particular point of view, but the nature of reality itself remains hidden from us. Although the scientist because of his methodology must speak of the world as inanimate "It,"

13. "Primary words do not signify things, but they intimate relations." Martin Buber, *I and Thou,* trans. Ronald Gregor Smith (New York: Charles Scribner's Sons, 1958), p. 3.

there is no guarantee that he speaks the full truth about the world. There are, in fact, reasons to believe that the component parts of the world, from the smallest atom to the largest star, participate in the "dimension" of egohood. Karl Heim writes:

> Here again, if we free ourselves entirely from the human per-
> spective, all that we can say with regard to this world of the small
> and ultra-small beings is that what takes place with the self-
> multiplying molecules, for example, is not necessarily merely 'a
> trace of sentience.' Just because it is unintelligible to us human
> beings, it is not necessarily any poorer than our own inner ex-
> perience. It is simply different from our human inner world. And
> so we must reckon with the possibility that this whole world of
> inorganic substances may also be an animate world. Then the
> saying in the Upanishads would be true: 'Soul alone is this
> universe.'[14]

Whether Heim's argument for this position is valid is a question which demands much more thorough investigation than we can engage in at this time. The only point which I wish to make is that our modern tendency to speak of the world as a collection of inanimate "Its" is not so much the conclusion of objective investigation as it is the unproved presupposition of scientific thought.

The second major fact which the mythologist discovers as he seeks to describe the "Powers" is that the "Powers" appear to man, as he exists in this world, not as one but as many. The ancient Hellenes, for instance, knew that although Aphrodite is an important "Power" in man's life she is not the only "Power." There are the old cosmological "Powers" of earth and sky, chaos and darkness which dominated for so long the life of man. These have, at least for the Hellene, been either defeated or transformed by the new gods, the gods of social order who won the day under the leadership of Zeus. Cronos remains, but his potency is gone, for Zeus has chained him. The earth goddess, Demeter, must still receive her due, but basically it is the "Powers" of govern-

14. Heim, *Christian Faith and Natural Science*, p. 102.

ment, the home, knowledge, sexuality, and so forth which shape man's destiny.[15] That these "Powers" are many goes without saying; to elevate one of them as *the* god should be regarded as a sign of either insanity or foolishness.

The third consideration is closely related to the second. Not only must the mythologist recognize the plurality of "Powers"; he must also accept the fact that these "Powers" do not seem to work in concert but continually vie with one another for man's allegiance. Human life is constantly threatened by the struggle between the gods, for in seeking to please one god man invariably displeases another. Agamemnon, to obtain favorable winds to sail to Troy, must sacrifice his daughter Iphigenia in order to satisfy Artemis. When he does so, however, he offends Hera and thus returns home triumphant only to meet his death at the hands of Clytemnestra. Orestes, in his turn, is called by Apollo to avenge his father. When he carries out this grim command he finds himself pursued by the dreadful Furies who protect the sanctity of womanhood. In the case of Orestes this struggle between the gods is ended by Athena, the goddess of wisdom, but man cannot always count on such good fortune.[16] He must act cautiously and without *hubris,* lest he offend a god or goddess and, as a consequence, find himself caught in a warfare which he cannot resolve.

## EGYPTIAN GODS

Thus far I have exemplified the nature of polytheism by referring primarily to the gods and goddesses of the Hellenic world. I have done so because these deities are more familiar to us and because they illustrate the meaning and nature of polytheism most clearly. In many respects, Egyptian mythology, though more closely related geographically and culturally to the exodus and Israel, is far more complicated and foreign to our ways of thinking. We may not approve of the Hellenic gods, pictured as they are as

15. Hesiod, in his *Theogony,* traces the development of these new powers.
16. Although Aeschylus's appeal to Athena's wisdom as a way of resolving the divine conflict seems to have appealed to Plato, Euripides repeatedly emphasized the inadequacy of human wisdom to bring man peace.

swashbuckling noblemen, but they are surely far more identifiable and understandable than the gods of Egypt who appear as a strange admixture of human and bestial traits.

Part of our difficulty in understanding Egyptian mythology is that the gods and goddesses of Egypt are closely tied to the particular geographic features of that land. Isis and Osirus are both connected with the life of the Nile and its gift of fertility to the soil. Set is obviously the manifestation of the dark and destructive powers of the desert. Even Rē, the sun god, is described from a thoroughly Egyptian point of view. He is the sun as it appears to Egypt, not to northern Europe or America. Since most of us are unacquainted with the Nile, the Egyptian desert, and the African sun, it is difficult for us to understand or appreciate the "Powers" being described.

This is not the only barrier to understanding Egyptian religion, however, for that religion embodies certain inconsistencies seemingly unfathomable to Western men. Not only does each god embody all sorts of apparently incompatible notions; it is also very difficult to establish what relation pertains among the gods. Horus, for instance, is described alternatively as the father, brother, and son of Osirus. Sometimes, different gods are used interchangeably to refer to the same reality. This does not mean the Egyptians had no sense of order. On the contrary, their world view was characterized by a profound sense of symmetry and uniformity.[17] Nevertheless, our Western, primarily Hellenic, standards of consistency are shattered by Egyptian mythology. We turn from Egypt either with a sense of sublime mystery, as did many Greeks, or with a sense of frustrating confusion.

On the whole, however, the interpretation of polytheism outlined briefly above applies just as well to the Egyptians as to the Hellenes. Essentially, we can say that they were trying to describe the various Powers and counter-Powers which had hegemony over the lives of the men who lived in the narrow fertile strip called

17. John A. Wilson, "Egypt," in *Before Philosophy,* ed. H. Frankfort et al. (London: Penguin Books, 1954), p. 50.

Egypt. If their description seems confused and inconsistent, it may be that this simply reflects the way in which the Powers actually affected men in the land of the Pharaohs.

One of the distinctive features of Egyptian mythology is the role played in it by the Pharaoh. In brief, the Pharaoh is equated with all the gods; he is said to be the power of the Nile, of the sun, of truth, and of justice all rolled into one. He is their incarnation; his will is an expression of theirs.[18] Although it may seem strange to us to call a living human being god, this was not at all repulsive to the Egyptians. Was not the Pharaoh truly the embodiment of Egypt? Was not his power supreme? Did he not define truth and execute justice?

Moreover, the centralizing of all diety in the Pharaoh was one way of solving, or at least minimizing, one of the basic problems of the polytheist. The difficulty with this form of religion is that when all is said and done it offers no moral or social unity for life. For the polytheist, life is struggle: struggle among the gods and struggle between man and the gods. The individual spends his life trying to appease the gods, trying to find some central value and destiny for his life. Inevitably he discovers that the integrated and happy life is impossible so long as Zeus and Aphrodite, Hera and Apollo war among themselves. When the situation is really seen for what it is, this sense of struggle leads inevitably to disillusionment with life, to acosmism, and to a flight to mystical release, nirvana, or perhaps narcotic hallucination.[19]

The Hellene attempted to account for the unity of existence by referring to Fate, but this only helped to accentuate the sense of purposelessness. The Egyptian, on the other hand, tried to solve the problem by making the Pharaoh the incarnation of all the gods. Integrity in life was sought by obeying this one god as the expression of them all. As noble an effort as this was, the strategy

18. Ibid., p. 81.
19. The rapid growth in the use of drugs in the twentieth century reflects modern, secular man's disillusionment with contemporary forms of what is actually polytheism and his yearning to escape the struggle.

was doomed to failure. The giving of all diety to the Pharaoh meant the development of an insufferable tyranny. Obedience to him brought a kind of integrity to life, but it was often the integrity of servitude and bondage. There were periods, of course, when this situation was modified. Many Pharaohs were mere ceremonial figureheads, so burdened with the ritualistic requirements of their office that they could not be tyrants in more than name. Nevertheless, society was organized from the top down and when the Pharaoh was a vigorous and strong-willed ruler, his tyranny could be fearful indeed. The pyramids witness to the vainglory of those deified men who enslaved millions to insure for themselves immortality.

Egypt's attitude toward the Pharaoh is important to keep in mind when the story of the exodus is read. The "king of Egypt" with whom Moses dealt was probably Rameses II, an energetic, ruthless, and tyrannical Pharaoh who seems to have exercised his powers to the full. He was a notable general, administrator, and builder to whose greatness testimonies were left all over Egypt.[20] For Egyptians, however, he was more than just an outstanding leader; he was god incarnate, the visible manifestation of all the Powers of Egypt. His defeat at the hands of the God of a mob of slaves, therefore, was of primary significance. It marked a revolution in human thinking far more dramatic than that produced by the conquests of Julius Caesar or the discoveries of Copernicus.

## 'ELOHIM

When we turn from the gods of the pagan peoples to the God of Israel, we enter a dramatically new world. The shift is so abrupt, so decisive, so earthshaking that it is difficult to comprehend. It is true that centuries of monotheism have blunted our understanding of what took place. We have come to take the concept of one God for granted. Nevertheless, when we return to the age of polytheism, learn to appreciate once more the truth

20. Gardiner, *The Land of the Pharaohs,* pp. 255–56.

of that universal faith, and then set off from Egypt for Sinai, the whole trek still seems like an overwhelming cataclysm.

Despite this radical turning point in the life of mankind which the exodus represents, there is still a kind of continuity which does exist between the mythology of Egypt and the faith of Israel. As we have already noted, this continuity is made evident by the very word which is translated in our English Bibles "God." *'Elohim* can mean both God and gods. If one can take this use of language seriously, it would appear that the Israelites regarded their God as *somewhat* (though only somewhat) like the gods of the pagans. The point of contact is to be found in the word "Powers." Both God and the gods are "Powers." While the pagan gods are many in number, however, the Lord of Israel is singular. He is the unity of all the "Powers" which manifest themselves in creation. All the various forces—the sun, the wind, the Nile, the plague—which were worshipped in Egypt as separate gods, find their source, reality, and unity in him. He is, in a word, all-powerful. As the Psalmist says:

> For the LORD is a great God,
>    and a great King above all gods.
> In his hand are the depths of the earth;
>    the heights of the mountains are his also.
> The sea is his, for he made it;
>    for his hands formed the dry land
>                                    (Psalm 95:3–5).

For modern man the basic theological question is usually stated to be, "Is there a God or isn't there?" For men of the ancient world, such a question would have been thought to be the height of foolishness. Obviously there are Powers which exert influence and control over man. To doubt the reality of such Powers would be to doubt the most certain fact of life. Hence, the question was not: "Does any God exist?" but rather, "Are there many gods or one?" Is the world merely a scene of cosmic conflict to which there is no solution, or is there, behind the apparent diversity, an ultimate unity? Ludwig Koehler in his *Old Testament Theology* writes:

> The assumption that God exists is the Old Testament's greatest gift to mankind. In the Old Testament God's existence is entirely a foregone conclusion, always presupposed; reference is continually being made to it; it is never denied or questioned.[21]

In one sense this statement is correct. Israelites offered no proofs for the existence of God. Atheism was, for the reasons explained above, no option for them. On the other hand, it is surely not the case that the men of the old covenant assumed without thought or temptation the unity of God. In fact, the history of Israel can be viewed as a struggle between those who believed in the unity of the powers in God and those who wished to revert to some form of polytheism. The real temptation which constantly confronted Israel was the temptation to doubt that all Powers flow from one transcendent deity. It is not difficult to believe that God is the source of the powers of righteousness, truth, and love, but is he also the source of plagues, earthquakes, and war? This is a question which we will discuss much more fully in chapter five. It suffices to say here that although the Bible officially promulgates the belief in one *'Elohim,* there are many evidences that Israelites found this faith difficult to maintain and repeatedly slipped back into one type of polytheism or another. The reason for this vacillation is clear. From a human point of view there seems to be no coordination of the "Powers" nor unity of purpose in life. The assertion that *'Elohim* is one rests not upon "common sense" but upon revelation. Israel's faith in the unity of God is based upon the fact that at certain moments in her life the hidden unity and purpose in life was revealed. When Israel forgot these revelatory events, a return to paganism was inevitable.

Israel, furthermore, did not engage in idle speculation. In fact, the prophets and apostles might well have been quite reticent to

21. From *Old Testament Theology,* by Ludwig Koehler, translated by A. S. Todd, p. 19. Published in the United States by The Westminster Press, 1958. © Lutterworth Press, 1957. Used by permission.

accept any arguments for the existence of God or proofs of what God is like in and of himself. They were quite well aware that once God is known as the "Powers" little more can be said univocally about God. *'Elohim* can only be described through metaphor and myth. They did know, however, that when they were confronted by him and when they praised him, they were compelled to use language appropriate for a person. They knew that to speak of *'Elohim* as an "It" would be to infer that God can be used and manipulated. And this was precisely what they knew was not and could never be the case. God is the one reality which cannot be turned into an instrument for human use. Man is made to dominate the earth, but he cannot dominate God. Therefore, he must address God as "Thou."

Does not this last sentence, however, seem to involve an inconsistency? If God is all-powerful, how can the earth exist apart from him? Does not man in using the powers of creation for his own benefit dominate God? In order to answer this obvious question, Israel developed and used the metaphors of creation. Through these metaphors she sought to express the twofold relation between God and the world.

On the one hand, Israel saw the world as totally dependent upon and as an expression of God. H. Wheeler Robinson points out:

> The Hebrew vocabulary includes no word equivalent to our term 'Nature.' This is not surprising, if by 'Nature' we mean 'the creative and regulative physical power which is conceived of as operating in the physical world and as the immediate cause of all its phenomena.' The only way to render this idea into Hebrew would be to say simply 'God.'[22]

If Robinson's interpretation is correct, Israel regarded the world itself as the manifestation of God. This is *mutatis mutandis,* what Buber means when he speaks of encountering "Thou" through a tree or other so-called physical object.[23] Not that the

22. H. Wheeler Robinson, *Inspiration and Revelation in the Old Testament* (Oxford: Clarendon Press, 1962), p. 1. Used by permission.
23. Buber, *I and Thou,* p. 7.

world itself is God, but the powers of the world are the direct manifestation of him.

On the other hand, Israel also knew that the world can be and, indeed, should be dealt with as an "It." Man is not commanded to fall in reverence before the individual powers of the created universe, but to dominate the earth and subdue it. Everything in the world is meant to be used by man for his own purposes. There are no sacred cows, no holy groves, no venerated mountains. Buber is certainly correct in reminding modern men that the world can reveal God, but he should also note more clearly than he does that one of Israel's primary contributions to the development of human thought was its demythologization and desacralization of nature. The first chapter of Genesis is one of the cornerstones upon which the modern scientific and technological world view is founded, for it presents the world as just the world and thus as controllable by man.

Although the Bible speaks of God's relation to the world in a variety of ways, two metaphors of creation underlie most of what is said. The first metaphor is embodied in the Hebrew word *yasar,* "he formed, he shaped." God is pictured as a potter at his wheel continuously shaping the earth.[24] Just as the shape of the pot is totally dependent upon the placement of the potter's fingers, so the "shape" of the world depends wholly upon God. As time proceeds, the potter's wheel spins on and the world continues to change its form according to the will of God. Thus creation is not final, but continues at every moment.

As long as one concentrates upon the shape of the artifact this metaphor is a useful one. If one asks, however, where the clay came from, it breaks down. Israel, unlike many other ancient peoples, seems to have had no conception of a preexistent "matter" which exists alongside of God but which was not created by him.[25] God is *not* seen to be like Plato's Demiurge who merely

24. See, for instance, Isaiah 29:16.
25. This, of course, is a point which is much debated among scholars, for Genesis 1 is ambiguous concerning this. The primary emphasis of Scripture, however, is upon the absolute sovereignty of God. There never is any reference to some recalcitrant matter as the source of evil.

imposes forms upon chaotic matter,[26] much less like Hesiod's gods who sprang themselves from chaos,[27] for to believe in preexistent matter would be to postulate some other "Power" beside the Almighty *'Elohim.*

No human metaphor can avoid the difficulty found in the metaphor of *yaṣar.* Man, as made in the image of God, can create, but his is always a qualified creation. He can create, but not "out of nothing." Nevertheless, the second metaphor used by Israel may come somewhat closer to the truth which the Bible attempts to convey. In the first chapter of Genesis, God is described as "speaking the world into existence." "And God said, 'Let there be light'; and there was light" (Genesis 1:3). God seems to be pictured as an ancient bard who creates simply through speaking. The world is God's poem which he continually chants. The past is but a tale which has been told; the future, but a song which has yet to be sung.

Within the tale, of course, the characters act with "independent consistency." Dorothy Sayers has pointed out quite illuminatingly that an author may create characters, but once they are created, they act with a kind of autonomy of their own.[28] The author who violates this autonomy by making his creations act "out of character" is an artless author. Moreover, an author can develop a personal relationship with his characters. He converses with them, experiences with them, laughs with them, cries with them. They may call him to continue his work and save them from their perilous situation. They may even convince him to alter somewhat his plan. Nevertheless, their destiny is in his hands; the denouement is his. Throughout the work he may offer hints, promises, and visions of what that destiny may be. He may offer to his characters hope and assurance. But above all, he must work out that destiny which he envisions in accordance with the integrity (or lack thereof) of the *dramatis personae.* They work

26. Plato, *Timaeus,* 48–50.
27. Hesiod, *Theogony,* 1.
28. Dorothy L. Sayers, *The Mind of the Maker* (New York: Harcourt, Brace and Co., 1941), p. 63 ff.

out their own salvation with fear and trembling; yet it is the author who works within them.

Although this metaphor comes somewhat closer to the doctrine of *creatio ex nihilo,* it is still imperfect. Even the bard who creates orally must use the air to communicate his thoughts. God, however, not only speaks his word; from him also proceeds the breath, the *ruah,* which makes his word communicable. The word *ruah* can be translated wind, breath, or spirit. Sometimes it is best understood in a purely physical way, as in Genesis 8:1 ("And God made a wind blow over the earth.") or Lamentations 4:20 ("The breath of our nostrils."). Often, however, it is used metaphorically to refer to the breath of God. God speaks and his *ruah,* his Spirit, proceeds from his mouth. Thus the communication of God's word depends upon his Spirit. This Spirit is not a part of the psychical makeup of man, for man depends upon God for the Spirit. When he receives that Spirit, he can hear God's word. When he does not, God's word to him is but garbled noise. Herein lies one of the mysteries of existence. Although God continues to speak his creative word, forming at every moment everything which is in the world, man does not always receive this word as word. He perceives the universe, but, because the Spirit is absent, does not know that every event is a word from God. Without the *ruah* the song of God, so pregnant with meaning, seems to be but endless, incomprehensible babbling, "a tale told by an idiot, full of sound and fury, signifying nothing."

### CONCLUSION

The biblical writers, unlike the Deists, did not conceive of God as a Power who once created independent substances which now operate independently according to their own laws. No thing (or better, no event) has any independent existence apart from him. He creates men who have wills of their own and yet who are at the same time an expression of the author who creates them. This is the central paradox of life; it is the mystery in which all men, if they could understand it, live.

Just when Israel developed a full "doctrine of creation" is difficult to determine. Undoubtedly it took many centuries to work out the vision of creation sketched in the first chapter of Genesis. Nevertheless, we find it in embryonic form each time the word *'Elohim* is used. Subtract the belief in one Almighty God from the story of the exodus and there is very little of significance left. From the beginning to end, the story of the exodus is the proclamation of the unity of the "Powers" in one transcendent, yet ever-present *'Elohim.*

We began this chapter with a search for a univocal statement about God which might serve as an anchor for our human metaphors about him. This anchor we have found in the word *'Elohim.* God is the "Powers"; he is expressed by the totality of all the forces which operate in the world and man. As the "Powers," God is transcendent, for he cannot be equated with any single force or event. Nevertheless, the power of reproduction, of the atom, of the army, of all things is his. To paraphrase the Koran, God is as close to man as the very vein on his neck.

At the same time, although God is the "Powers," his reality cannot be reduced to just the sum total of all the forces in the universe. These forces express his will; yet God, the transcendent creator, remains hidden. Just as a person is known to other men through his body, so God is recognized as the "Powers." In this sense his reality is indubitable. But just as that same person is hidden from men "behind" his body as a transcendent, self-conscious ego, so God too remains hidden. Only as he reveals himself through the "Powers," his objectively experienced aspect, can his will for man be grasped.

## Chapter 3

# ISRAEL AND THE WORD

Since we have already discussed the metaphor of divine "speaking," the assertion that "God spoke" should not appear strange to anyone who has followed the argument thus far. For Israel, every event—and the world is composed of events—is a word from God. In fact, such a belief is built into the Hebrew language, for the word *dabar* can signify not only a word but a promise, a saying, a thing done, an affair, an event, a thing, a cause. The Israelite would not say as we do, "Actions speak louder than words." He would say instead, "Actions are words which speak plainly what we mean."

This is particularly true concerning God's speech to man. Although the Bible describes a number of ways—dreams, visions, angels—through which God communicates his will, the most important means is through what might be termed meaningful events. The events of history are objective "tokens" which convey, either potentially or actually, God's will for man. The fact that God continually speaks, however, does not mean that man necessarily hears and understands. On the contrary, most people, though confronted by God's word-events, do not understand them at all. The series of events called the world and history is like a tablet containing what looks like ancient hieroglyphics. The question which perennially faces man is: Are these words or merely random scratchings? There is a kind of consistency about them which would seem to hint at some meaning, but what that meaning is remains undecipherable until some Rosetta stone is found which gives a clue to the correct translation.

The Psalmist speaks of this situation when he writes:

> The heavens are telling the glory of God;
>   and the firmament proclaims his handiwork.
> Day to day pours forth speech,
>   and night to night declares knowledge
> > (Psalm 19:1–2).

In effect he proclaims that the world is made up of the self-identifying words of God. To this believer the whole earth sings the praises of God. Still, he goes on:

> There is no speech, nor are there words;
>   their voice is not heard;
> yet their voice goes out through all the earth,
>   and their words to the end of the world
> > (Psalm 19:3–4).

The voice of the world may go out, but to him who does not have the key to understanding, the words are incomprehensible. Man can see and know the sun who "like a strong man runs its course," (19:5) but how can he know God?

The Psalmist's answer is clear and straightforward:

> The law of the LORD is perfect,
>   reviving the soul;
> the testimony of the LORD is sure,
>   making wise the simple;
> the precepts of the LORD are right,
>   rejoicing the heart
> > (Psalm 19:7–8).

In other words, it is the Torah of God and, in particular, the special word-events to which the Torah witnesses which illumine and make meaningful the whole poem of God which we call creation. Israel did not begin by rationally deducing the existence of

God from the existence of the world as did, say, Thomas Aquinas. Neither did she find God, as William Wordsworth said he did, in the beauties of nature. No, Israel encountered God in certain special word-events in her life and, as a result, came to hear God's word everywhere.

No word-event has been more illuminating for Israel than the event of the exodus from Egypt. Whenever she wishes to speak of the God she worships or of the meaning she finds in life, Israel returns to the exodus to glorify the God who brought her out. Therefore, if we are to understand Israel's faith, we must hear this word spoken in the exodus.

Such a task is by no means simple or easy. In the first place, the word which Israel claims to have heard is not a set of ready-made propositions to which the hearer is expected to assent through an act of "intellectual acceptance." The exodus event is rather like a *Gestalt* which is either seen or not seen. To use the terminology of Ian Ramsey, it is a "discernment situation" in which the light suddenly dawns.[1] The story is told, not just to communicate facts, but to produce in the hearer that moment of discernment when he says, "Now I see." No amount of thinking or meditation will necessarily produce this response.

The believer, then, can by no means prove that an intelligible word is spoken in the event at all. The most that he can do is to point to the event and say, "This is where I and a host of others have heard God speak. This is not just my subjective opinion; many have heard God speak here. Listen carefully and you may hear him also." The unbeliever can put himself in a position where such a moment of discernment may take place. Until discernment occurs, however, he will be like a color-blind man trying to appreciate the beauties of a sunset.

The problem of hearing the word is complicated for modern men because of the historiographical questions which we inevitably ask. We want to know whether the events really happened

1. Ian T. Ramsey, *Religious Language* (New York: Macmillan Co., 1957), p. 19 ff.

as they are described. We want to know what elements of the story are original and which were added later. These are good and interesting questions which must not be suppressed, for historical reconstruction in itself is a worthwhile task. The problem is, however, that in our historical research the word heard by generations of Israelites may well elude us. The primary question for one wishing to hear the word should be not "What really happened?" but "What meaning does this story convey? Toward what discernment does this story-point?" In other words, the story of the exodus must be approached as "literature," as a unified narrative which attempts to communicate to the reader a truth which surpasses both the positivistic statements of the historian and the systematically wrought doctrines of the theologian.

This is not to say that objective historical analysis and higher criticism are useless. Both are significant enterprises, but they simply are not effective ways to arrive at the meaning of the text as it stands. By insisting upon "objectivity" historiography attempts to circumvent the witness of the later generations and therefore circumvents as well the word to which these generations witness. Documentary or source criticism attempts to distinguish and isolate the "voices" of Scripture but in so doing tends to destroy the tension and harmony among the voices from which discernment emerges. Perhaps, then, those theologians of the past who argued that one must accept Scripture just as it stands were not as foolish as is often thought. Insofar as they refused to give objective historiography and higher criticism their due, they may have been misguided. Nevertheless, as theologians and religious men, they were quite right in pointing to the Bible itself as the "place" where the light dawns.

## THE EVENT

Israel, according to the Bible, had entered Egypt when Joseph was in power but had, after his death, been enslaved by a new king who "did not know Joseph" (Exodus 1:8). There they existed for several generations—the text is not entirely consistent about the length of time—in bondage.[2] Into this situation Moses, the son of Levite parents, was born. Moses, though an Israelite, somehow escaped this bondage and was brought up as a son of the Pharaoh's daughter, but was forced to flee from the land when he killed an Egyptian taskmaster. His flight took him to Midian where he became a shepherd, tending the flocks of his Midianite father-in-law in the desert of Sinai.

In the midst of this desert, near a mountain called Horeb, the first of a series of strange incidents took place. Moses saw an amazing sight: a bush (or perhaps a crag)[3] that burned but was not consumed. Through this event he was reminded of the plight of his people and heard God's choosing word. We shall return in the next chapter to a closer analysis of this word-event.[4] It suffices to say here that as a result, Moses returned to the Egypt from which he had fled to persuade the Pharaoh to let Israel go free.

Moses arrives in Egypt armed with certain "magical tricks" not unlike those of the Egyptian magicians. He can turn a supposed stick into a snake and make his hand appear leprous. Both of these feats impress the Israelites, but are scarcely sufficient to convince the Pharaoh that he should release a fairly sizable number of workmen who are constructing store-cities for him. After all, his own magicians can perform the same type of trick. Hence, in response to Moses' request he gives a flat "No!"

There then follows a series of incidents which, if taken singly, might cause little commotion but which, taken together, are most astonishing. Ten times Moses returns to the Pharaoh to seek his approval for the departure of the people of Israel. Ten times the refusal of the Pharaoh is followed by what we might term today a "natural disaster." The Nile turns bloodred; frogs hop out of the water and die; swarms of gnats and flies come; the

2. Infra, pp. 93–96.

3. *Gesenius' Hebrew and Chaldee Lexicon to the Old Testament Scriptures,* ed. Samuel Prideaux Tregelles (Grand Rapids, Mich.: Wm. B. Eerdmans, 1954), p. 591.

4. Infra, pp. 73–79.

cattle die and the Egyptians are afflicted with boils. Then a hailstorm strikes the land, followed by a plague of locusts and a thick darkness (a dust storm?) which lasts for three days. Finally, a plague striking down the firstborn sweeps the land, killing even the firstborn son of the Pharaoh himself. Throughout all this, Israel remains unscathed.

At last the Pharaoh agrees to let Moses and his people go and they depart across the desert. No sooner are they out of his sight, however, than the Pharaoh changes his mind and sends his troops after them. The doom of Israel appears sealed. Behind her are the rapidly approaching Egyptians; before her is the apparently impassable Sea of Reeds.[5] Just when it appears that all hope is gone, the Egyptians are delayed by what appears to be a dust storm and a wind parts the water of the Sea so that Israel can cross. And so the people escape to the other side and freedom. When the Egyptians attempt to follow, their chariots are mired in the mud, the water returns and many are drowned.

Modern readers often label these stories as miraculous and regard them as examples of Israel's belief in the supernatural intervention of God in the natural order. It is significant, however, that the Bible does not speak of miracles but of '_ot_ or "signs." This is a better term for, in truth, most of the events described are not in and of themselves "supernatural" at all. There is nothing "unnatural" about a plague of locusts or frogs. Even the "Sea of Reeds" incident can be understood as a natural event. The wind simply blew and uncovered a way across an otherwise seemingly impassable marsh.[6] Moreover, it must also be

---

5. G. Ernest Wright, *Biblical Archeology* (Philadelphia: Westminster Press, 1957), pp. 61–62. It is noteworthy that the new translation of the Torah published by the Jewish Publication Society uses the term "Sea of Reeds" rather than the more traditional, but incorrect "Red Sea."

6. The wind might well have blown hard enough to reveal a ridge of fairly solid earth across a marsh. This area was drained when the Suez canal was built and, therefore, there is no possibility of reconstructing what happened with any precision. It is true that some accounts of the story do mention a wall of water standing on either side. This embellishment may well be due to the influence of Canaanite mythology on the memories of Israel. See: Frank E. Eakin, Jr., "The Reed Sea and Baalism," *The Journal of Biblical Literature,* December, 1967.

noted that the Israelites did not think in terms of the "natural" and the "supernatural." God, for them, could not intervene in nature, because he was regarded as the source of the powers of nature. Everything that happens happens according to his will. Every plague, every dust storm, every wind is a manifestation of his creative power. What made these events unique was that they happened just when they did. Just when Israel needed the plagues they occurred as Moses said they would. What we might call a "coincidence" they called an *'ot,* a sign that God was acting. Thus the story of the exodus is a *Gestalt* through which one realizes that all of the powers of creation are a manifestation of the one *'Elohim.* For a moment the ambiguous curtain of experience is lifted and one sees all things working together for the good of Israel.[7]

In the tenth plague the coincidental aspect of these events is heightened in the extreme. Although both a plague and the death of a firstborn son are natural, in this plague only the firstborn of the Egyptians are affected. The person who concentrates only upon the historical probability of the event, misses the meaning of the story. Is not its point that in the exodus many suffered so that the firstborn son of God, Israel, might go free? Is this not the inner meaning of the exodus in which so many generations of Israelites have rejoiced?[8]

There is also another, complementary meaning to be found in this narrative. Not only does the story proclaim that all of the powers worked together to lead Israel out of Egypt, it also reveals Israel's faith that all of the gods of the pagans are illusory. The

7. I do not mean to imply that this discernment can be reduced to a simple statement about the unity of the powers in one God which can be accepted by the intellect alone. This *Gestalt* demands a response of faith with the whole self. It requires not only intellectual comprehension but personal commitment as well.

8. It is interesting to observe that while the old Passover emphasizes the suffering of the many for the one, the "new Passover" (Easter) involves the suffering of the one for the many. From a Christian perspective, the old Passover finds its *telos,* its fulfillment and completion, in the death and resurrection of Jesus.

river god, the Nile, turns bloodred. Rē, the sun god, is darkened.[9] Even Set, the destructive god, works for the Lord of Israel. The story thus reveals that though there are many powers, these powers are ultimately one. Even the Pharaoh, the unity of the Egyptian gods, is but a pawn in the hands of 'Elohim. His heart is hardened, his son killed, his troops defeated. He is shown to be only a finite man and not a god at all.

The truth which the book of Exodus reveals, then, transcends the historicity of any particular event. It is an assertion of the faith that God is totally in charge, that there are no forces which operate apart from him, and that he has acted both to free and choose Israel. This is the truth which generations of Israelites heard in the exodus event and sought to express in the narrative which we are studying.

The temporarily suppressed question of the modern historiographer must now be allowed to surface. Did these events really occur? Had I been there, would I have experienced them? Jack Finegan, in his book *Let My People Go,* struggles valiantly to prove that the Bible is historically accurate in the modern, positivistic sense. In particular he seeks to show that none of the plagues needs to be considered "supernatural." Most of his arguments are based upon the ideas of Greta Hort whose conclusions he takes as his own and whom he quotes as saying:

> We have found that each of the plagues in its essential features describes correctly a natural phenomenon, which, though far from common, may yet happen in Egypt from time to time. Moreover, with the exception of plague No. 7 we have also found that each of the plagues follows directly or indirectly but always necessarily from the first plague and in the sequence described in the Bible. We have further found that the range and manner of cessation of each plague coincide with that of the natural phenomenon described. . . . The conclusions prove that the Bible gives us an historically accurate account of the ten plagues, and,

9. Egyptians hated darkness particularly; it was for them a symbol of death. John Wilson, in *Before Philosophy,* ed. H. Frankfort et al. (London: Penguin Books, 1954), p. 53.

unless we are willing to credit E or some predecessor of his with a most intimate knowledge of life in Egypt and with having transferred a series of events which he himself had witnessed to Mosaic times, we must also conclude that the Biblical account gives us true and historically accurate information of the events which led up to the Exodus of Israel from Egypt.[10]

In one sense this argument as summarized by Finegan is quite impressive. Although it is not true that we *must* conclude, as Finegan does, that the Bible gives us a historically accurate picture, his arguments should cause those who accept the radical surgery performed on the text by the documentary critics to reconsider their position.[11] Nevertheless, the whole argument is predicated upon a distinction which is wholly foreign to the biblical way of thinking.

Finegan seeks to prove that the ten "plagues" can be accounted for "naturally." The point of the biblical teaching about creation, however, is that there is no distinction between the natural and the supernatural. From a biblical point of view one cannot speak of an independently operating order called nature, unless one wishes to equate nature and God. It is true that the biblical writers did distinguish God and what we perceive as the world around us. Creator and creation are not the same, but because creation depends at every moment of its existence upon God, it has no immutable laws of its own by which it must operate. Therefore, it would have been more appropriate for Finegan simply to argue that in doing what he did in Egypt God acted with consistency. He did nothing which he had not done before and might not do again.

The question, however, is not whether these events could have happened, but whether they did, in fact, occur in a way which could have been observed by anyone present. Usually a historian, faced with such a question, answers it by referring to informa-

10. Jack Finegan, *Let My People Go* (New York: Harper and Row, 1963), p. 56.
11. Martin Noth, *Exodus, A Commentary* (Philadelphia: Westminster Press, 1962), pp. 67–84.

tion available from other sources. In the event that no such information is extant—as is true in this instance—the historian bases his decision upon probability. That is to say, he asks himself whether, given our knowledge of the consistencies inherent in the natural order, the occurrence of such an event seems probable. The problem is complicated by the fact that the Israelites themselves indicate that these events are highly improbable. Indeed they are mentioned because the improbability of such a series of coincidences caused the people to regard them as a special sign. Hence, to doubt that the plagues occurred as they are described because such coincidences are improbable, is to beg the question.

The literary critic usually seeks to circumvent this problem by analyzing the book in order to identify the various sources which compose it. Thus the plagues are often doubted because they are attributed to a late source. When examining the arguments of most of the higher critics, however, one finds oneself again in a circle. The plague stories are regarded as late because they are "obvious legendary accretions."[12] In other words, the question is answered by presupposing the answer. Furthermore, even if the passage describing the plagues is considered "late" because of its form and language, there is no guarantee that it is not based upon much earlier stories.

Thus, it would appear that we are left with no firm ground upon which to come to either a positive or a negative conclusion. Perhaps the most that we can say is that something happened at the time of the exodus which led Israel to affirm that her God is the Lord of all creation. There must have been some sign which led the people to believe that the exodus was not just a matter of luck or coincidence but was caused by God himself. The believer who discerns in the book of Exodus the voice of God is free to doubt the originality of this or that specific occurrence. What he is not free to deny and remain true to the biblical faith is that the God of Israel is the Lord of creation who causes to pass

12. Ibid.

all that comes to pass. Although the story of the exodus *may* not be historical in any positivistic sense, it nevertheless reflects, far better than any merely factual account could, the word-event heard and witnessed to by Israel throughout her long history. The truly significant historical fact is that Israel heard God's word in this narrative of events and, as a result, believed herself to be chosen for his special purposes.

## AFTER THE SEA OF REEDS

The chain of signs and wonders does not end with Israel's crossing of the sea into freedom. While in the desert, the people of Israel run out of water and cry out against God for bringing them into the wilderness to perish. Moses, in response, takes his rod and strikes a rock from which pours forth water. Surely, one might say, this is more than just a coincidence; this is a supernatural miracle. We know today, however, that the rocks of that desert are porous limestone and sometimes contain sizable pockets of water. In recent times, thirsty travelers in the desert have found water in the same way.[13] What is strange is that Moses was able to find such a pocket of water just at the moment when it was needed most. Again, it is the coincidental nature of the event which makes it a sign.

The same type of "natural" explanation can be given for both the manna and the quail. Even today a sticky, sweet substance secreted by a certain type of insect on the Sinai Peninsula is sold in Cairo. This is probably what Israel called manna.[14] The finding of quail has also been "explained." Doubtless these were migratory quail such as still fly south over the area to warmer climes. They fly over the desert until exhausted and then drop, almost lifeless, upon the desert floor. Because of their exhaustion, they can be picked up quite easily.[15] What was strange about the event was

13. Wright, *Biblical Archeology,* p. 65.
14. Ibid.
15. Ibid.

not that the quail were caught but that they happened to appear when Israel needed them.

Quite obviously, however, the significance of the events is not exhausted when one has explained them "naturalistically." The point of all of these three passages is that "man cannot live by bread alone." Rather all bread comes from the hand of God. Israel survived in the desert because God cared for her. Whether or not Israel really ate manna in the wilderness is an interesting historical question, but it is somewhat beside the point. Insofar as Israel truly remembered this event, she experienced it over and over again. Throughout her history, Israel was "fed" by God's gift of manna in the desert. The fact that it is possible that originally these coincidences did not occur exactly as they are recorded says nothing about the truth of the faith which the narrative expresses.

Finally, after three months of travel, the people of Israel arrive at the mountain where Moses had previously seen the burning *seneh* and had been called by God. The fact that it is exactly "on the third new moon after the people of Israel had gone forth out of the land of Egypt" (Exodus 19:1) is underlined in the text by the words "on that day" which follow immediately. Doubtless great significance was found in this "coincidence" for both the number three and the new moon were of special importance to ancient men in general and to Israel in particular.[16]

With their arrival the fulfillment of the sign promised to Moses at the burning bush seems at hand. God had said to Moses:

> But I will be with you; and this shall be the sign for you, that I have sent you: when you have brought forth the people out of Egypt, you shall serve God upon this mountain (Exodus 3:12).

Now that sign has become a reality; Moses *had* indeed been sent by God. But why? Why had God called Israel out of Egypt? What destiny lies before this band of freed slaves encamped before the mountain? What word of meaning has God spoken in the strange

16. Ernst Cassirer, *The Philosophy of Symbolic Forms,* trans. Ralph Manheim, 3 vols. (New Haven: Yale University Press, 1955), 2: 150–51.

events which had released Israel from bondage? It is time for Moses to reflect and he ascends the mountain to hear what God has said and is saying to Israel.

## THE EAGLE SPEECH

The message which Moses receives from God is brief; yet its significance can hardly be overestimated. In but a few sentences, the essential meaning and purpose of the word spoken by God to Israel in the exodus are clarified.

> Thus you shall say to the house of Jacob, and tell the people of Israel: You have seen what I did to the Egyptians, and how I bore you on eagles' wings and brought you to myself. Now therefore, if you will obey my voice and keep my covenant, you shall be my own possession among all peoples; for all the earth is mine, and you shall be to me a kingdom of priests and a holy nation. These are the words which you shall speak to the children of Israel (Exodus 19:3-6).

Why has Israel been able to escape Egypt? Why have so many unaccountable "coincidences" occurred which have enabled her to avoid the Pharaoh's chariots and travel in safety through the dangerous desert? It could not have been just luck! The one God, the God who controls all the powers of this world has done this. He has borne her gently but swiftly as an eagle bears its young as it teaches them to fly, that she might meet him here. He has chosen Israel, he has set Israel apart, just as the tales concerning the patriarchs say. From all of the peoples of the earth, Israel has been singled out to be God's treasure, his *segulah*. This ragtag army of escaped slaves who are not even all Israelites (Exodus 12:38) he has chosen as his portion from the earth. This band of gripers and recalcitrants he has selected to be his priests, his mediators in the world!

It is noteworthy that even at this moment, when God's word of election is most clearly heard, when Israel suddenly knows herself to be set apart for a special destiny, the world is not forgotten. God is not conceived as just a tribal deity or mountain god. He is

'Elohim; the whole earth is his. Israel is not chosen simply for her own benefit. No, Israel has been led out in order that she may serve God's purposes among all men. Her task, her calling, her purpose is not to start just another religion for the few or to serve God in an obscure way. Rather her task is to be *in the world* as a kingdom of *kohanim,* of priests. She is to be the sign of faith in the midst of a floundering humanity. Her sacrifices, her praise, her prayers are not to be offered just for herself. Israel is set apart as holy so that she may intercede for the world and finally bring all of humanity to God.

It is true that this vision of Israel's destiny has been sometimes, perhaps often, forgotten by the people of God. There have been times when in her pride Israel has thought she was chosen because of her own righteousness. There have also been periods when, because of Israel's tenuous situation in the world, this destiny has appeared as but an unbelievable dream. Nevertheless, it was from this seed that Israel's hope for the future grew. The belief that Israel is the priesthood of mankind is really the source for her messianic hopes and eschatological dreams.

This motif does not occur in the Decalogue itself, but it must not be forgotten when the Ten Commandments are studied. It is the positive purpose which lies behind the apparent negativity of the commandments. The reason why the Ten Commandments of God are to be obeyed is so that Israel may serve as the priest of God. The Decalogue is the discipline of the priesthood, the means whereby the mediation will take place. To think that the "Law" stands over against the ministry of reconciliation as something to be overcome is to misunderstand the whole point of God's speech to Israel.

Mention should also be made of the meaning of the words "obey" and "keep" which are found in the Eagle Speech. The word *šama'* which is translated "obey," means more literally "to hear." Since the form used is intensive, the text might be translated, "If you really and truly hear my voice." That is to say, if you hear God's covenantal word with all your heart, mind, and strength, then you shall be God's treasure. *Šamar,* the verb which is translated "keep" also has a slightly different meaning in the Hebrew. *Šamar* does indeed mean "to keep," but in a very positive sense, for its primary meaning is "to guard or to watch over." Keeping God's covenant, then, is an active response, like watching sheep or even tending a garden. It means to be ever wakeful and alert, guarding God's covenant as you would your most precious possession. This, then, is no call to blind obedience or passive submission to some heteronomous laws laid down by a divine tyrant. It is a call first to meditate upon the events of Israel's life so that God's word may speak clearly through them and then to guard that meaning from all corruption.

After the Eagle Speech which Moses hears from God and delivers to the children of Israel, Israel agrees to accept God's covenant. To them, at least at this moment, there is no doubt; God has led them out from Egypt with signs and wonders. Therefore, they will harken to what he has to say and will keep his covenant. Moses knows, however, that before they can hear God's covenantal word, they must prepare themselves. The covenant is nothing which can be entered into flippantly. Therefore, for three days Israel prepares herself to meet God. Moses performs acts of cultic consecration; the people wash their garments and avoid sexual intercourse to ready themselves to "hear."

### THE VOICE IN THE THUNDER

On the third day after the third new moon, a most auspicious time for ancient men, an extraordinary event occurs. The book of Exodus describes what happened in the following way:

> And Mount Sinai was wrapped in smoke, because the LORD descended upon it in fire; and the smoke of it went up like the smoke of a kiln, and the whole mountain quaked greatly. And as the sound of the trumpet grew louder and louder, Moses spoke, and God answered him in thunder (Exodus 19:18–19).

Exactly what took place is still a matter of some debate among scholars. Some have maintained that the mountain, being a volcano, erupted. The problem with this view is that there are no volcanic mountains located in the Sinai Peninsula. If the text describes an eruption and if it is "factually accurate," this would place Mount Sinai somewhere in Arabia. Although such a location is possible, it calls into question the route of the Israelites described in Exodus. Others maintain that what is described is a severe thunderstorm or an earthquake. I would suggest that both of these latter theories are correct. Again, just on schedule, what modern men might call a "natural coincidence," occurred. A thunderstorm broke out at the same time that some tremors shook the region. It is no wonder that the people are described as afraid and are said to have heard God speak in the thunder. If we accept the interpretation of the way God speaks which has been presented, that is a good way to put it. Here, in this unaccountable concatenation of events, God makes himself known. This is the capstone, the culmination of the whole exodus experience, the final clinching event through which the word becomes clear and manifest.

Israel's "translation" of this word of thunder into human speech is found in Exodus 20. Just when this translation was made is an open question. Some claim that the original band of Israelite escapees heard these words in the word of thunder; others argue that the Decalogue, at least in its present form, was only developed after years of thought and meditation upon the event. Unfortunately there is no easy way to settle the issue. What is important is that generations of Israelites have understood the word of thunder as making precisely these demands upon Israel and in turn have agreed to accept these words as a basis for their covenantal agreement with God.

## "AND GOD SPOKE ALL THESE WORDS"

As Solomon Goldman has pointed out in his excellent work on the Ten Commandments, the structure of this sentence in Hebrew is rather unusual.[17] In all other instances in the Bible, a sentence

17. Solomon Goldman, *The Ten Commandments*, ed. Maurice Samuel (Chicago: University of Chicago Press, 1956), p. 124.

of this kind includes an indirect object. Hence, one would expect it to read, "And God spoke to Israel saying." Why the recipient of these words is not named is unclear. Is it because Israel only came into existence after hearing these words? Is it because God is pictured as speaking to the whole world, to all who have ears to hear? Is it because the word Israel was simply inadvertently omitted from our text? We do not know. It is one of those linguistic peculiarities which may one day be explicated but which now remains obscure. In any case, as the sentence stands, the emphasis falls upon *kol-hadebarim ha''eleh,* "all these words."

Although we have become accustomed to speaking of the Ten Commandments, it is interesting that the book of Exodus speaks not of commandments but of "words." This may not seem to be a very important distinction, but the use of *debarim,* words, rather than *misot,* commandments, does change the flavor of the passage somewhat. It means that these are not just authoritarian commands delivered from on high, but meaningful "words" which are heard in the strangely propitious events of the exodus. Just as the word of the exodus is a word of deliverance and hope so these words are words of joy as well, for they are bearers of meaning as well as duty.

According to the Talmud these ten words were first spoken by God as one utterance, namely as what is identified by Jews as the first commandment, and from this word were derived all the rest.[18] Although this idea may appear at first glance to be a bit of rabbinic obscurantism, there is more profundity here than meets the eye. From the event itself comes the Word, "I am the LORD your God, who brought you out of the land of Egypt, out of the house of bondage" (Exodus 20:2), and from this are derived all the other commandments. What God speaks is one word; what Israel hears is ten. From this one event she derives the ten essential words which govern and give meaning to her life. Our task in the exposition which follows is to discover how each of

18. Ibid., pp. 125–126.

these words is related to the primary word and what meaning each derivative word has.

Before we can embark upon this task, however, a few questions might be posed concerning the ordering of these ten words. Why are there exactly ten commandments? One common answer is that there are ten commandments because men have ten fingers. For the purposes of memorization, one commandment is assigned to each finger. This explanation seems quite plausible, but it would be equally easy to justify other numbers.

As a matter of fact, there are some who believe that originally there were not ten commandments anyway. These scholars argue that at the beginning the number was somewhat smaller and that commandments were added as time went on.[19] Even many of those who do believe that the original list contained ten commandments think that at first the commandments were more abbreviated than they are now.[20] It is often stated quite categorically that the justifying phrases such as are found in the second, third, fourth, and fifth commandments were added later to explain the meaning and purpose of the particular "word."

This, of course, may have been the case. The more I study the commandments, the more convinced I become that these words were not put together haphazardly but are the product of many centuries of "hearing" of God's voice and meditating upon it. There are no wasted words or rough corners. Every word is in its proper place. This may imply, however, that originally there were more than ten commandments or that the commandments once were longer than they are now. In other words, one could argue that the process of development was one of refinement and abbreviation rather than one of expansion and elaboration. The fact of the matter is we do not know how these commandments took shape. Equally good arguments can be given for the position (a) that the commandments are retained the way they were

19. Theophile James Meek, *Hebrew Origins* (New York: Harper and Brothers, 1950), pp. 37–38.
20. Noth, *Exodus, A Commentary,* p. 161.

originally heard, (b) that the commandments have been increased in number or augmented in length, or (c) that they have been the product of refinement and distillation. The whole question, for our purposes, is somewhat beside the point. What is important is that for centuries Israel has returned to this word-event to hear precisely these words of meaning. For generations, they have been considered by the faithful to be an adequate translation of what God speaks in the thunder.

One of the most perplexing features of the Ten Commandments is that although virtually everyone agrees that there are ten words spoken by God, there is no universal agreement about how the commandments are to be divided one from another. According to Jewish tradition, verse two constitutes the first commandment; verses three through six, the second; verse seven, the third; verses eight through eleven, the fourth; verse twelve, the fifth; verse thirteen (verses thirteen through sixteen in Christian versions), the sixth, seventh, eighth and ninth; and verse fourteen (seventeen in Christian versions), the tenth. Roman Catholics and Lutherans, on the other hand, treat verse two as the preamble, count verses three through six as the first commandment and then treat verse fourteen (seventeen in Christian versions) as two. Greek Orthodox and Reformed Churches choose still a third path, treating verse two as a preamble, separating verse three from verses four through six as two commandments, and then treating verse fourteen (seventeen) as one.

To many modern scholars the last option seems to be the most reasonable of all, for it is difficult to consider verse two by itself as a commandment or verse fourteen as two commandments. Furthermore, verses three through six do seem to contain two distinguishable commandments which can be appropriately treated separately. Although it can be argued that to have other gods and to make graven images of them are really the same action, it also seems quite feasible to treat these as different enough to warrant separate prohibitions. Thus, I shall treat the commandments according to the usage current in Greek and Reformed Churches.

One cannot be absolutely dogmatic on this question, however. The Jewish tradition is old and venerable and must not be cast aside because it does not seem to provide quite so neat an arrangement. If one begins with the idea that the first word is the fountainhead of all the rest and thinks of it as a "word" rather than as a commandment, then the Jewish tradition concerning the division of the Decalogue is understandable and acceptable. At any rate, this is ultimately a minor point which should not concern us unduly, for it does not appear to affect too much the exegesis of the commandments whether one adopts one formulation or another.

# PART II:

# YAHWEH

"I am the LORD your God, who brought you out of the land of Egypt, out of the house of bondage.

You shall have no other gods before me.

You shall not make for yourself a graven image, or any likeness of anything that is in heaven above, or that is in the earth beneath, or that is in the water under the earth; you shall not bow down to them or serve them; for I the LORD your God am a jealous God, visiting the iniquity of the fathers upon the children to the third and the fourth generation of those who hate me, but showing steadfast love to thousands of those who love me and keep my commandments.

You shall not take the name of the LORD your God in vain; for the LORD will not hold him guiltless who takes his name in vain."

## Chapter 4

# ISRAEL AND YAHWEH:
# A PREAMBLE

"I am the LORD your God, who brought you out of the land of
Egypt, out of the house of bondage."

## "I"

The Decalogue *per se* begins with what might be called the most
shocking word in the whole Bible. We are accustomed to speak of
God in the third person, as a "He," in whom we believe. Martin
Buber has reminded us that the word "He" is really not sufficient
to express man's profoundest relation to God, for it implies an
"I-It" relation. Since God is not a manipulatable "It," Buber
speaks of "I-Thou" as a more appropriate word to express the true
relation between man and God.[1] As correct as this position may
be, the Bible goes one step further. Israel not only stands at the
foot of the mountain and utters a primordial "Thou," God himself
speaks, confronting Israel with his own "I." God speaks his *'anoki*
bluntly and forcibly through the whole event of the exodus.
Through signs and wonders he addresses Israel until she cannot
but hear the Power of the universe saying, "I am."

I have said that this is a shocking word, and so it is if

1. Martin Buber, *I and Thou,* trans. Ronald Gregor Smith (New York:
Charles Scribner's Sons, 1958), p. 75 ff. This is one of Buber's primary
emphases throughout this work.

contemplated with candor. It means that the Power which governs the planets in their courses, causes water to evaporate and vegetation to blossom, makes the human heart beat and the human mind think is a Power who can and does identify himself with the word "I." This "I" does not simply stand over against us; this "I" surrounds us, envelops us, constitutes us. This is the "I" which cannot help but disturb, indeed overwhelm us, if it is heard at all.

In the light of this "I" of God, the reality of all other "I"'s must be reconsidered. Having heard God's word of self-identification, we can no longer speak our own "I" with unqualified assurance, for if the Power of the universe says "I", what does it mean for us, finite creatures, to say the same? This is the mystery in which man stands. It is the enigma of both sin and redemption. Logically, there can be but one "I" in the universe, for any reality apart from "I" is non-I. Nevertheless, God says "I am" and yet addresses Israel as Thou, as a Thou united with and yet somehow set apart from himself, as a Thou who can also say "I." God is all in all; yet he has granted to his finite creatures a kind of independence which allows them to stand over against him and speak a personal word in response. Israel is finite; yet, though she is the expression of the will of the Powers, she must stand apart from the mountain from which he speaks, listen to his voice and respond to his word with an "I" of her own.

As Karl Heim has so persuasively pointed out, one of the chief causes for conflict in this world is the existence of a multiplicity of egos.[2] Each man, although self-transcendant, sees the whole universe from one particular vantage point. The world, by definition, revolves around him. Since more than one ego exists, however, this multiplicity of centers inevitably leads to conflict. Egos confront one another and struggle with each other for the mastery of existence. Worlds collide as egos strive to hold the center of the stage which they each believe to be rightfully theirs.

2. Karl Heim, *Christian Faith and Natural Science* (New York: Harper and Brothers, 1957), p. 67.

The revelation of the ego of God alters this situation decisively, at least in principle. If God says "I," then my own ego cannot be the center of the universe. I must cease to struggle with others and acknowledge instead the centrality of God. Thus the word "I," when spoken by God, forms the basis for true righteousness among men. As long as each human ego believes itself to be the center of the world, ethical theory and practice can only be a rationalization for personal or corporate self-interest.[3] Only when the "I am" of God breaks down the claims of the human ego can true righteousness flower, and the Scylla and Charybdis of relativism and fanaticism be avoided.

## "THE LORD"

Since the "am" of the prologue is implied rather than expressed in the Hebrew, we shall pass immediately to the covenantal name of God here revealed. "The Lord" is a rendering, but by no means a translation of the Holy Tetramegon, YHWH, spoken by God. Instead, "the Lord" is a translation of the word *'Adonai* which pious Jews came to read instead of YHWH after the latter became thought of as too holy to pronounce.[4]

Although the name Yahweh is used throughout the Torah to refer to God, it is here employed in a particularly significant way. God is making a covenant with Israel and so reveals to her the covenantal name by which he will henceforth be known. In doing this God does not deny the use of other names. Israel may still name her God *'El Šaddai,* or *'El 'Elyon,* or *'El Kana',* but his

3. This may seem to be an unjustified generalization. Surely, however, the classical types of ethical theory (Epicureanism, Stoicism, Aristotelianism, and even Platonism) are all based, in one way or another, upon self-interest as the primary motivation. Later ethical theories developed in Western culture are not so easy to categorize for most have been influenced by the Judeo-Christian tradition. Furthermore, it must also be admitted that the heirs of this tradition have also appealed, sometimes rather blatantly, to personal self-interest.

4. For generations Christians misunderstood the Hebrew text which contains the consonants of YHWH but the vowels of *'Adonai* and thus read the name as "Jehovah." Today scholars are generally agreed that the name should be transliterated not by such an impossible Hebrew word but by the word Yahweh.

covenantal name, the name through which Israel enters into covenantal relation and in which she will henceforth live, is now revealed to be Yahweh.

This is not the first time that God has spoken this name in the exodus story, for it is one of the names which God revealed to Moses at Mount Horeb, when he saw the burning bush. There is some question, however, whether this name was first used by Moses after this theophany or whether it had a longer history of use in Israel. Numerous scholars argue that, although Yahweh is used as a name for God throughout Genesis, one source for the Torah regarded it as a name revealed first to Moses. A number of facts are presented to support this point of view. First, it is noted that Moses, at the burning bush, does not begin by naming God Yahweh but instead asks for the name of the God who addresses him. This would seem to indicate that the name Moses receives is a new one. Second, this idea seems to be borne out by God's word to Moses in Exodus 6:2–3:

> And God said to Moses, "I am the LORD. I appeared to Abraham, to Isaac, and to Jacob, as God Almighty, but by my name the LORD I did not make myself known to them."

This sentence is interpreted as proving quite conclusively that, at least to the author of this passage, Yahweh was a new name which had been unknown to the patriarchs.

Apparently not all of the writers of the Bible so believed, however, for the name Yahweh is used quite freely in many passages of Genesis and, in fact, is said to have originated very early in the history of mankind, at the time of Seth and Enosh (Genesis 4:25–26). Thus Yahweh is seen to be a name used not only by Israel but by other peoples as well. Since some passages say that the name was used from earliest times while others imply that the name was not known until the time of Moses, it would seem that a basic inconsistency exists in the Torah concerning the use of the name Yahweh. On the basis of this inconsistency, among other things, the documentary critics distinguish the

Yahwist document (which uses the name Yahweh throughout) and the Elohist document (which does not use the name Yahweh until after the revelation at Sinai). Because such an important scholarly theory is based upon this inconsistency, it is necessary to examine the text with care to test the validity of this interpretation.

Let us begin by returning to Exodus 3 and Moses' confrontation with God at the burning bush. It is significant, first of all, that God does not begin by identifying himself as Yahweh. Rather he confronts Moses by saying, "I am the God of your father, the God of Abraham, the God of Isaac, and the God of Jacob" (Exodus 3:6). Why God identifies himself initially as the God of Moses' own father is perhaps an important, but at this time unanswerable, question. What is significant for this discussion is that he does not identify himself as Yahweh until Moses begins to raise objections to his calling.

God calls Moses to return to Egypt to set Israel free, but Moses exhibits great reluctance. "Who am I that I should go?" he protests. God tries to reassure him, saying that he will be with him, but Moses raises a second objection. "If I come to the people of Israel and say to them, 'The God of your fathers has sent me to you,' and they ask me, 'What is his name?' what shall I say to them?" (Exodus 3:13). In order to understand the full significance of this question it must be remembered that according to the book of Exodus, Moses, before returning from Midian, was not very closely associated with the people of Israel. Although he was nursed by his mother when a child and apparently retained some sense of kinship with the Israelites when he grew up, he was brought up in the Pharaoh's household. Moses, then, is raising what appears to be a serious objection to God's plan. How can Moses be persuasive among the people of Israel when he does not even know the name of their God? Moses seems to be asking, not for a new and unknown name, but for a name which is already known to the people of Israel.[5]

5. Martin Buber, *Moses, The Revelation and the Covenant* (New York: Harper and Row, 1958), pp. 48–49.

While Moses' question seems simple, God's response is not.

> God said to Moses, "I AM WHO I AM." And he said, "Say this to the people of Israel, 'I AM has sent me to you.'" God also said to Moses, "Say this to the people of Israel, 'The LORD, the God of your fathers, the God of Abraham, the God of Isaac, and the God of Jacob, has sent me to you': This is my name for ever, and thus I am to be remembered throughout all generations (Exodus 3:14–15).

A number of questions are raised by this statement by God. First, why does God offer to Moses three names rather than one? It is true that *'Ehyeh Ašer 'Ehyeh* ("I am who I am" or "I am that I am"), *'Ehyeh* (I am), and Yahweh are linguistically related, for Yahweh is probably the third person, hiphil form of *hayah,* the same verb used in the other two names. Nevertheless, these are three distinct names which are not really interchangeable. One answer which commends itself is that while God himself can say *'Ehyeh Ašer 'Ehyeh* or *'Ehyeh* of himself, Israel can hardly speak in the first person singular of God. God is the "I" of the universe, but when Israel speaks of him, she must speak in the third person. Thus Moses in speaking to Israel uses the name Yahweh.

Second, we must ask what these names, or these varieties of this one name, mean. Although they are all forms of the verb *hayah,* one should not read into them a Platonic conception of "being." *Hayah* can be translated "to be" but it can equally well be rendered "to fall out, to happen, to come to pass, to become."[6] In other words, since Hebrew offers no clear distinction between being and becoming, one should not interpret these names as implying any conception of static or timeless being.

Furthermore, some scholars argue that these names seem to be in the hiphil or causative form, and therefore suggest that God's name should be translated, "He causes to pass what comes to pass." Others argue that the form is future and thus translate

6. Francis Brown, S. R. Driver, and Charles A. Briggs, *A Hebrew and English Lexicon of the Old Testament* (Oxford: Clarendon Press, 1959), p. 224.

God's name, as he speaks it himself, as "I will be what I will be" or "I will manifest what I will be" or "I will manifest what I will manifest."

The first thing to recognize is that Yahweh is a name which is rich in meaning. It is one of those enigmatic names which can be, and perhaps was meant to be, understood in a variety of ways. If so, there is no one "correct" translation. Rather, the name reminds the hearer of the splendor and mystery of God. He is, will be, and causes to pass what comes to pass all at once. No matter what the meaning, the implication is that Moses is given a name which will be recognized by the people of Israel. If this is a correct understanding of this passage, however, it would appear to conflict with Exodus 6:2–3 in which, as it has already been stated, God says that he did not make himself known to the patriarchs by the name Yahweh.

The question is, what is meant by the sentence, "but by my name the LORD I did not make myself known to them"? The verb *yada'*, of which *noda'ti* (I made known) is a niphal form, can be translated "to know"; yet as usual the Hebrew has different connotations from the English. For instance, Lot, in Genesis 19:8 says, "Behold, I have two daughters who have not known a man." Surely Lot does not mean that they have never made the acquaintance of a man. No, he means that they have never engaged in sexual intercourse. By the same token, the people of Israel might have been acquainted with the name, Yahweh, without truly "knowing" it.

An even more persuasive example is found in Jeremiah 16:21. The prophet says, "Therefore, behold, I will make them know, this once I will make them know my power and my might, and they shall know that my name is the LORD." Certainly Jeremiah does not mean that the people of Israel in his day are unaware that their God is called Yahweh. Rather he means that although they are acquainted with the name, they do not know it in the deepest sense, for they do not obey Yahweh's covenant.

These two examples show quite convincingly, I think, that Exodus 6:2-3 does not necessarily imply that the name Yahweh was not used before the exodus. Instead, it means that now, as a result of the event of the exodus, the name will be known in a new and deeper way. This interpretation is borne out by a closer analysis of the context in which this passage is placed. Moses has already gone before the Pharaoh to demand that the people of Israel be let go. Instead of complying with this wish, the Pharaoh has only made the plight of the Israelites worse, demanding that they not only make bricks from straw, but that they themselves find the straw for the bricks. As a result the foremen of Israel complain first to the Pharaoh and then, with great bitterness, to Moses and Aaron. Moses, in turn, calls upon Yahweh to justify himself for this evil which has befallen Israel (Exodus 5:22-23). Yahweh responds:

> "Now you shall see what I will do to Pharaoh; for with a strong hand he will send them out, yea, with a strong hand he will drive them out of the land." And God said to Moses, "I am the Lord. I appeared to Abraham, to Isaac, and to Jacob, as God Almighty *('El Šaddai)*, but by my name the Lord I did not make myself known to them. I also established my covenant with them, to give them the land of Canaan, the land in which they dwelt as sojourners.
>
> Moreover I have heard the groaning of the people of Israel whom the Egyptians hold in bondage and I have remembered my covenant. Say therefore to the people of Israel, 'I am the Lord, and I will bring you out from under the burdens of the Egyptians, and I will deliver you from their bondage, and I will redeem you with an outstretched arm and with great acts of judgment, and I will take you for my people, and I will be your God; and you shall know that I am the Lord your God, who has brought you out from under the burdens of the Egyptians. And I will bring you into the land which I swore to give to Abraham, to Isaac, and to Jacob; I will give it to you for a possession. I am the Lord" (Exodus 6:1-8).

In brief, the meaning of this passage may be summarized as follows: Be patient and you will see what I will do. Until now you have really only known me fully as *'El Šaddai*. Now through the events which are to come to pass, you will come to know the meaning of my name, Yahweh. Tell the people that I shall lead you out, make you my people, and bring you into the land which I promised to your fathers. When you have experienced these events, then you will know what it means to call me Yahweh. In other words, the revelation of the name which took place at Horeb, was not the revelation of a new name but the beginning of the revelation of a new significance of an old one.

It may seem peculiar, however, that God says that he revealed himself to the patriarchs as *'El Šaddai,* for this name is used only six times in the whole book of Genesis. Nevertheless, the importance of this name must not be underestimated. In two of the four instances that God introduces himself by name (Genesis 17:1 and 35:11) he uses the name *'El Šaddai.* On the other two occasions (Genesis 15:7 and 28:13) he uses Yahweh, but both of these cases may be suspected as emended texts. The Septuagint version of Genesis 15:7 reads *theos* rather than *kyrios* and may, therefore, indicate that the original text used *'Elohim* or perhaps even *'El Šaddai.* Genesis 28:13 does read Yahweh and there is no textual variations which imply that this was not the original reading. Still, when Jacob, in Genesis 48:3 refers back to the theophany of Genesis 28, he says that *'El Šaddai* appeared to him and blessed him. This may well indicate that in an earlier version Jacob's vision at Bethel was a revelation of the name *'El Šaddai* rather than of Yahweh.

Even if the texts of Genesis 15:7 and 28:13 stand, *'El Šaddai* still occupies a peculiar position among the names of God used in Genesis because of its unique association with the rite and covenant of circumcision. God, of course, makes several covenants in the book of Genesis and in making them he does not always use the name *'El Šaddai.* The covenant made between God and Abraham in Genesis 17 is of particular significance, however, because God, who speaks of himself here as *'El Šaddai,* demands of Abraham a responding act, namely circumcision. It is quite probable that the rite was performed in the name of *'El Šaddai* and thus was the physical revelation of the meaning of that name. If that is so, Exodus 6:3 might be interpreted as meaning: "I revealed my covenantal name to your fathers to be *'El Šaddai,* but by my name Yahweh I did not seal my covenant."

What did this earlier covenantal name mean and how does it differ in meaning from Yahweh? Usually this name is translated "God Almighty" and, in a philological sense, this may be appropriate, if somewhat arbitrary. The usual justification for this translation is found in the purported relation between *Šaddai* and the verb *šadad,* to be strong or powerful. It is significant, however, that in the book of Genesis *'El Šaddai* is invariably associated with sexual fruitfulness. The only possible exception to this generalization is to be found in Genesis 43:14, but even here it can be argued that the association with the power of procreating offspring is not farfetched.

If *'El Šaddai* is associated with the power of procreation, there is some reason to suspect that originally *Šaddai* may have come, not from *šadad,* but from *šadah,* "to cast forth, shoot, or pour out," a word with overt sexual connotations.[7] I do not mean to imply that the patriarchs worshipped only the power of sexuality, but Genesis does indicate that God revealed himself to them primarily, though not exclusively, through the commandment to be fruitful and multiply and through the sometimes almost unbelievable gift of children. His promises to them invariably entailed some hope that their offspring would be numerous. It may be that the patriarchs thought they would take over the land of Canaan simply by increasing in number through procreation. In

7. This is, of course, a highly speculative suggestion which is by no means accepted by most scholars. The majority seem to regard Albright's argument that *Šaddai* means "of the mountain(s)" (*From the Stone Age to Christianity,* [Garden City, N.Y.: Doubleday Anchor Books, 1957], p. 244) as definitive. Nevertheless, the close association between *'El Šaddai* and procreation in Genesis is clear. If *'El Šaddai* originally meant "God of the mountains," this name surely took on new signification for the "authors" of Genesis, for there is no indication that they thought of the God of Abram as a mountain deity.

the exodus, however, God reveals to Israel a new name. No longer is he to be thought of as primarily the giver of children, though this remains an important function. Through the exodus he reveals himself to be he who brings Israel out of Egypt, as he who saves by causing to pass what comes to pass. Just as Israel came to know the name *'El Šaddai* by entering into the covenant of circumcision, so now Israel comes to know his new covenantal name by entering into the covenant at Sinai.

For centuries Semites had used this name. Buber suggests that originally the name may have come from the very primitive utterance Yah, Yah, Yah: He, He, He.[8] There is also some evidence of a linguistic relationship between the name Yahweh and the Canaanite god YW.[9] Now, as Israel stands at the foot of the mountain she comes to a new understanding of this name which had long been on her lips. As the earth quakes and the thunder sounds she stands face to face with the very Power of existence and knows, by committing herself to this power, the name which is above all names, Yahweh.

### "YOUR GOD"

If the "I" of this sentence is a shocking proclamation of a startling truth, the "your" is hardly less so. There have been many philosophers in the past who have argued for a "personalistic" understanding of God and have agreed that God does say "I," at least to himself. Few, however, have found it easy to believe that this "I" who is the unity of all the powers in the universe not only could but has so committed himself to a people that he can identify himself as *their* God. This, nevertheless, is the kind of

8. Buber, *Moses,* p. 50.

9. Edmund Jacob, *Theology of the Old Testament,* trans. Arthur W. Heathcote and Philip J. Allcock (New York: Harper and Row, 1958), p. 49. Jacob regards Dussard's view that the single mention of YW in the Ugaritic texts (VI AB, col. 4, l. 14) indicates a relation between El and Yahweh as unproved. So, indeed, it is. The very use of this divine name may, however, indicate a pre-Mosaic knowledge of the name among pagans.

God which the Bible proclaims. The power who makes E equal MC², who expresses his will in the mysteries of DNA, and who propels the subatomic particles in their courses is also the Power who has said, "I am the LORD *your* God" to Israel.

This does not mean that Yahweh is a nationalistic God who will defend Israel right or wrong. As God points out in his Eagle Speech in chapter 19, all the earth is his; every nation is chosen for a special role in the history of the world. Nevertheless, Israel's particular destiny is not like that of the other nations. She is Yahweh's special portion among the nations; she is to be his emissary and his priest. Other nations may do his will, but they are unaware that it is his will that they do. In contrast, Israel is conscious of her calling, for she has stood at Sinai and heard his voice. In a word, God and Israel have covenanted together.

The idea of a covenant is by no means peculiar to Israel, for people in the ancient Near East made covenants of all sorts. Business contracts, political relationships, marriages, and many other types of human relations were regularized and made official through the making of a covenant, a *berit*. G. E. Mendenhall has examined covenantal forms used by the Hittites and has demonstrated that Israel's covenantal agreements were of much the same form.[10] Still, the frequency with which the idea of a covenant occurs in the books of Genesis and Exodus is striking. The God of Genesis, indeed, may well be described primarily as a covenant-making God. Furthermore, the nature of these early covenants is rather surprising. Never do the patriarchs plead with God that he should covenant with them. Instead, God invariably arrives quite unexpectedly to bind himself to a patriarch with a promise of progeny and/or land. More often than not he does not even ask for any particular response on the part of the recipient. He does not say: "I will give you this land if you do this and this and this." Instead he categorically states, "For all the land you see I will give to you and to your descendants forever" (Genesis 13:15).

10. G. E. Mendenhall, *Law and Covenant in Israel and the Ancient Near East* (Pittsburgh: Presbyterian Board of Colportage, 1955), passim.

One must grant that God does provide the rite of circumcision as a sign of the covenant and does test Abraham by demanding that he sacrifice Isaac on Mount Moriah, but these demands come after the fact. Had Abraham refused to go, the promise would have remained.

In this sense, at least, the covenant made by God with Israel at Sinai is unique. It is true that God does take the initiative throughout. Israel does not win her freedom from Egypt; God gives it to her. Nor does Israel in any way win the right to covenant with God; God offers his covenant to her freely. The Law is based upon the good news that Israel is released from Egypt, not vice versa.

Nonetheless, this Sinaitic covenant is different from the other covenants made with the patriarchs for there is a "string attached." "Now therefore," says God, "if you will obey my voice and keep my covenant, you shall be my own possession among all peoples" (Exodus 19:5). I have already argued in chapter three that it is illegitimate to interpret this sentence in a legalistic way. What God demands is not just blind obedience to a set of rules and regulations but attentiveness and the constant cultivation of his covenantal word. Still, he does demand and Israel, in turn, accepts these demands. No longer is this a one-way relationship. In responding, Israel becomes a covenantal partner. She takes upon herself the responsibility of faithfulness and in so doing becomes a "person."

Without these demands, without this structure for her life, Israel would have no real identity or destiny. The law is essentially a call to fidelity and is based upon the good news of deliverance. In its turn the law gives that gospel of deliverance substance and meaning. Without the word of good news, the law would be only an imposition of a legal burden. Without the commandments, however, the good news would soon become empty and of little consequence. The demands of the covenant are an aspect of God's grace. Without them Israel would remain an "it." The word "you" demands reciprocity.

Before the Sinaitic covenant, Israel was bound together by only the ties of blood. With this word Israel now becomes a people, an *'am*. According to Exodus 12:38 not only the family of Israel but a "mixed multitude" went out from the land of Egypt. Therefore, though Yahweh came only to the lost sheep of the house of Israel, he saved others from bondage as well. Nor is there any indication given that this mixed multitude did not take part in the covenantal agreement made at Sinai. Apparently they, too, vowed to hear and keep God's word and thus were grafted into Israel. Israel became not just one family held together by a common ancestor but a people united by a common hearing of God's word. One of the tragedies of Israel's history is that she often forgot this fact and assumed that Israel's unity was to be found only in her bloodline. The New Testament is a reaffirmation of the ancient truth that Israel is a people who hears and obeys rather than simply a family which procreates.

Before the time of the exodus it would appear that the central metaphor used to describe Israel's relation to God was the metaphor of sonship. For instance, when God sends Moses to Egypt, he says to him,

> "And you shall say to the Pharaoh, 'Thus says the LORD, Israel is my first-born son, and I say to you, "Let my son go that he may serve me"; if you refuse to let him go, behold, I will slay your first-born son' " (Exodus 4:22–23).

This metaphor was a good way to describe Israel's relation to *'El Šaddai,* for in Genesis he is conceived as the Power who brought Abram out of Ur and who gave him sons and the promise that his offspring would be numbered like the stars of the heavens. The covenant at Sinai, however, could not very aptly be described as the initiation of a father-son relation, since such a relation was already in existence. Hence new metaphors were formulated to describe this new relation between Israel and her God. The idea of the fatherhood of God was not wholly forgotten but receded into the background as Israel developed new ways to speak about her covenantal relation with Yahweh.

During the years following the covenantal act made at Sinai the people of Israel developed several characteristic ways of speaking about that covenant. Among the metaphors which were used three can be singled out as most important:

1. God is King: Israel is his kingdom.
2. God is Master: Israel is his servant.
3. God is Husband: Israel is his wife.

Each of these metaphors appropriately describes some aspect or aspects of the covenantal bond. No one of these figures is wholly satisfactory taken by itself, but together they approximate the fullness of the relationship which was initiated at Sinai.

## GOD IS KING: ISRAEL IS HIS KINGDOM

The motif of the kingship of God is found throughout the Bible. Its importance for the covenant is underlined by the reference to it in the Eagle Speech in Exodus 19:6: "And you shall be to me a kingdom of priests and a holy nation." Although this idea is not mentioned explicitly in the Decalogue, it is clearly evident throughout the rest of the Torah. It is God, the king, who guides Israel in the desert with his pillar of fire. It is God, the king, who sets forth the basic law for Israel and determines difficult judicial cases through the sacred lot and the various trials "by fire." It is God, the king, who leads in battle, firing Israel with the courage of his Spirit and striking fear into the hearts of the enemy.

This kingship, implies Scripture, began with the Sinai covenant. Before that time God had aided Israel and made promises to her; now he is enthroned a king of the people. Moses may be God's spokesman, but it is Yahweh who sits invisibly upon his throne, the ark, meting out his judgments and leading the people in battle. Nor is this just a picturesque and poetical metaphor with no practical implications. The belief that God is *melek* in Israel had profound political and social consequences which distinguished Israel from most, if not all, of her neighbors.

Because the kingship was ascribed to God alone, human leadership always took, at least in theory, a secondary place. Moses is described as a great leader, but he is never glorified as a hero or demigod. His faults are portrayed honestly, the punishment of his sins recorded, and his grave carefully hidden from those who might, at some later time, wish to turn it into a sacred shrine. Moses, far from being considered a king, is normally described as an *'ebed,* a slave of the Lord.

Perhaps it was for this reason that Israel retained the "democratic" nomadic spirit for so long. Even those passages in the Torah written after the development of the human kingship in Israel contain no statutes commanding obedience to some political leader. Israel's obedience is to God alone, not to any human potentate or king. This meant, in the early days, the lack of any centralized form of government. Justice was administered by tribe and through various charismatic leaders (judges) who were called by God to lead Israel in times of trouble. Although the elders of a given community or tribe were considered men of authority, they were apparently not regarded as dictators. Moreover, the *ruah* (Spirit) of God could transform even a woman such as Deborah or a brigand like Jephthah into a judge and leader of the people.

In many ways, this effect of the belief in the divine kingship was salutory. There was, for several centuries at least, no centralized tyranny in Israel such as dominated most other nations of the ancient Near East. This meant that there was considerable liberty so that, as the book of Judges says, "every man did what was right in his own eyes" (Judges 21:25). Unfortunately, however, the kingship of Yahweh also tended to produce, albeit illegitimately, a kind of disunity among the tribes which left Israel as a whole weak when faced by foreign invaders. Even at the time of Deborah there were complaints that not all the tribes had joined in the fight against the common foe (Judges 5:16–18).

By the time of Samuel such a problem had become severe. The Philistines threatened the very life of Israel as a nation and, therefore, despite the strong protests of Samuel, the people cried for, and finally received, a king.[11]

With the victorious rule of David, the kingship was firmly established as a human institution. As Samuel saw very clearly, although this kingship provided a kind of security which the old charismatic leadership could not offer, it also meant the loss of certain liberties which Israel had long cherished. There was great danger that David would become but another oriental potentate. That this did not quite happen, at least not immediately, is a testimony to the power of the traditional belief that God is *melek* and that no human can rightfully usurp his authority. In any other oriental country the king's seduction of another man's wife would have been considered tolerable if not quite within the bounds of propriety. Nathan's pointed accusation, "You are the man,"[12] was a reminder to David that God was still the real *melek* in Israel and that even David came under his judgment. That David accepted this judgment and repented is a tribute both to David's wisdom and to the power of the tradition.

Unfortunately, David's successors tended to forget this important motif and therefore brought all kinds of trouble upon themselves. When Rehoboam tried to play the oriental potentate, he lost more than half his kingdom and split for centuries the nation of Israel. The spirit of nomadic democracy rang through the land: "What portion have we in David? To your tents, O Israel!" (1 Kings 12:16). Henceforth, because God was not given his due, there were two human kings rather than one.

There was also another danger inherent in the metaphor of the kingship which fostered even greater problems. Perhaps it was this danger which led to its gradual, though by no means complete, decline. The idea that God was king for Israel not only

11. 1 Samuel 8–9. The anointing of Saul as king of Israel doubtless marked one of the important turning points in the history of that people.

12. 2 Samuel 12:7. This story of Nathan's open criticism of David is a classic example of the prophet's relation to the king.

led to political chaos; it also could, and sometimes did, lead to the deification of the state. In other words, this metaphor was falsely construed to mean that God was on the side of Israel and that he would fight for her against all her political enemies. Through this perversion of the original idea, God, the power of the universe, became god, the political power of Israel. This, of course, was to turn God into an idol and to make nonsense out of the whole theological tradition of Israel, and for this reason, it was strongly resisted by the prophets. They knew, as some modern scholars do not, that the God of the covenant is a universal God, "the Powers." Because of the obvious political advantages for the political leaders and the need for security on the part of the people, however, there was a constant danger that Yahweh would be understood as being like the gods of the other nations, that is, as an embodiment of national power and self-interest whose main task was to defend the interests of a particular people. In this development the king became more and more the embodiment of both Israel and the will of God. The king's position as the "son of God" who had the right to call Yahweh his father illustrates that this was by no means a minor danger.[13]

It was against this perversion of the concept of the divine kingship that the prophets protested continually. The prime object of their attack was the identification of the nation's will with God's will. Again and again they emphasized that Israel stands under divine judgment and faces punishment for her sins. They did not abandon, however, either the idea of the kingship of God or the human kingship of the Davidic line. Rather they attacked the human kingship of their time by proclaiming the absolute kingship of God, holding up the hope for a divinely ordained king of the future. This hope, as is well known, played a vital

13. 2 Samuel 7:14. "I will be his father and he shall be my son." Yahweh here speaks to David concerning his son, Solomon. "Son of God" undoubtedly became one of the titles of the king (see Psalm 2:7). Thus the king was regarded as the epitome of Israel, and the firstborn son of Yahweh. This use of the title should be kept in mind when reading the New Testament.

role in the development of the new Israel, Christianity. Jesus is proclaimed to be human and yet the manifestation of the divine kingship. His kingdom is at hand; yet it transcends all human authority. Unfortunately, the Christian church has all too often been tempted to circumvent, in one way or another, the dialectical nature of Christ's kingship. The church has, at various times, been identified as the kingdom of God and thus has been regarded as exempt from divine judgment. As a consequence, the universal *'Elohim* has been replaced by an idol, the power of the church. Protestantism has, in theory, rejected such idolatry but, in practice, has often succumbed to the same temptation.

## GOD IS MASTER: ISRAEL IS HIS SERVANT

The idea that Israel is the servant of God is not as prominent in the Torah as the idea that Israel is his kingdom, but it is there nonetheless. For instance, the word *'abad* which means "to work or serve in the way that a slave serves his master" is used to refer to the worship of God. Hence, when a man worships God he serves or "slaves for" him. If this metaphor can be taken literally, the covenant which is expressed in part through worship is then conceived of as a legal act through which Israel voluntarily takes upon herself the role of the slave of Yahweh.

In some ways, this is a fitting metaphor, for it expresses the sense of absolute fidelity which God demands of his people. This is no business contract between equals in which only the letter of the law is to be obeyed. The Master, who is totally in control, demands obedience to the spirit of the law as well.

Despite the fact that Deutero-Isaiah raised this metaphor to great heights in his portrayal of Israel as the servant of God,[14] this way of describing Israel's relation to God has some obvious limitations. Although slavery was accepted among Israelites as a part of life, it was generally regarded as degrading. The condition of slavery was one which was to be escaped, not enjoyed.

14. See e.g., Isaiah 42:1–4, 44:1–5.

Furthermore, the pagan peoples also used this metaphor to describe their relation to their gods. The Canaanite title for God, *Ba'al,* meant, in fact, "Master." Therefore it is not surprising that Hosea, who so bitterly attacked Canaanite paganism, prophesied:

> "And in that day, says the LORD, you will call me, 'My husband,' and no longer will you call me, 'My Ba'al.' For I will remove the names of the Ba'als from her mouth, and they shall be mentioned by name no more" (Hosea 2: 16–17).

This does not mean that Hosea rejected this metaphor completely. Still, it shows with what distaste the idea of God as Master came to be regarded.

## GOD IS HUSBAND: ISRAEL IS HIS WIFE

The quotation from Hosea also introduces us to the third metaphor used by Israel to describe the covenant, for he pictures Yahweh as Israel's husband. Although this idea is not clearly mentioned in the Torah, there are some strong suggestions that this view of the covenant is not wholly absent from the book of Exodus, and, in particular, from Exodus 20. For instance, the words used in the second commandment for love and hate strongly suggest this marital motif.[15] Certainly elsewhere in the Bible the vocabulary used to describe Israel's relation to Yahweh is laden with marital connotations.

With the prophets, particularly with Hosea, the metaphor of marriage becomes explicit and central. Hosea, however, gives no indication that he is using a new image when he speaks of Israel as God's unfaithful wife. On the contrary, he seems rather to be employing, albeit in a most shocking way, an idea already well known by his people when he marries a prostitute in order to reflect God's relation to Israel. If the people of his day were not already well acquainted with the idea of Israel as Yahweh's wife, Hosea's message would have made little sense at all. Thus it is

15. Infra, pp. 122–127.

certain that this idea antedated Hosea and may indeed have been very ancient.

In any event, it became, as time went on, a very significant way of speaking about God's relation to Israel. This is clearly shown by the use made of the metaphor by Jeremiah and Ezekiel and by the fact that the Song of Songs, a thoroughly erotic piece of love poetry, was included among the Megillot[16] as the scroll to be read at the festival of Passover. If we are to understand how later, and perhaps early, Israelites thought of the covenant we must examine this metaphor with care.

Despite its initially rather startling character, one can understand why the marriage metaphor came to be regarded as one of the best ways of describing what happened at Sinai. In many respects, it makes more sense of the whole biblical narrative than any other analogy used, for it expresses both the exclusiveness and personal character of the covenant in a very impressive and beautiful way. Perhaps the most striking feature of the whole covenantal tradition is the particularity of God's choosing love. Out of all the *goi'im* of the earth, God selects Israel to be his treasure. Neither of the other two covenantal metaphors can quite express this motif of personal commitment or the sense of covenantal joy. The whole story of Genesis from chapter 12 on can can be understood as a long betrothal period culminating, after years of waiting, with the marriage at Sinai. Yahweh pledges his love to Israel through his promises to the patriarchs and then, when she is enslaved, redeems her so that the long-planned marriage can take place.

Of course, as in any marriage, certain formal vows are made. God, like a good Israelite husband, promises to be faithful to his wife and to give her her rightful *meena,* the land. He vows to provide for her and protect her from all harm and danger. He

---

16. Megillot is the name given to the five scrolls included in the Writings, the third part of the Old Testament. Each is read on a specific feast day: Song of Songs, at Passover; Ruth, at Pentecost; Lamentations, on the Ninth of Ab; Ecclesiastes, at Tabernacles; Esther, at Purim. Together, these scrolls present a beautiful description of the many-sided nature of man's life and experience.

also makes certain formal demands upon his wife which she must fulfill to be considered a good wife; she is called to love, honour, and obey. Although absolute, these vows are not harsh burdens imposed but the foundation upon which the structure of love can be built. Despite the fact that the I-Thou of Exodus 20:2 is in some ways similar to the I-Thou of a Hittite suzerainty treaty,[17] the metaphor of marriage reveals that it has the force of the I-Thou of the modern formula, "I, John, take thee, Nancy."

Although Hosea's use of this metaphor to describe Israel's infidelity and God's forgiving love is beautiful and impressive, it is unfortunate, in some ways, that it was he who first made the metaphor explicit. The image of Israel's marriage to God is one of great joy and gladness, for Israel is called to love and delight in her husband. Hosea quite rightly emphasizes how perverted this relationship has become in his time, picturing Israel as a nymphomaniac who inevitably goes whoring after other gods. What was meant to be an image of exhilarating happiness becomes for him a word of woe and destruction. Hosea goes on to speak of God's continuing love and of Israel's hope for future marital happiness. Still, the image takes on connotations of doom which are mitigated only by Yahweh's "Nevertheless."

The same is true of the use made of this metaphor by Jeremiah and Ezekiel. Hosea likens Israel to an unfaithful wife and prophecies an imminent separation which will be overcome only by God's love. Jeremiah heightens the ominous nature of Israel's situation by speaking of the inevitability of divorce.

> "If a man divorces his wife and she goes from him
> and becomes another man's wife, will he return to her?
> Would not that land be greatly polluted?
> You have played the harlot with many lovers;
>     and would you return to me?
>                         says the LORD"          (Jeremiah 3:1).

Finally, this prophet does see hope for Israel in the future, but he knows that simple repentance and reconciliation are not

17. Mendenhall, *Law and Covenant*, pp. 30, 37.

enough. Therefore, he prophesies that God will make a new covenant with Israel (Jeremiah 31). Restoration of the old covenant is insufficient; God must marry Israel again with a new covenantal act.

In some respects, Ezekiel goes even further than Jeremiah in his assessment of the end of the old covenant. His use of the marriage metaphor is extraordinarily harsh.

> Wherefore, O harlot, hear the word of the LORD: Thus says the LORD God, Because your shame was laid bare and your nakedness uncovered in your harlotries with your lovers, and because of all your idols, and because of the blood of your children that you gave to them, therefore, behold, I will gather all your lovers, with whom you took pleasure, all those you loved and all those you loathed; I will gather them against you from every side, and will uncover your nakedness to them, that they may see all your nakedness. And I will judge you as women who break wedlock and shed blood are judged, and bring upon you the blood of wrath and jealousy (Ezekiel 16:35–38).

The penalty for adultery, of course, was death. Ezekiel, therefore, seems to be saying that the penalty for Israel's sin will not be divorce, but execution. Hence, when he speaks of Israel's hope for the future he speaks not so much of a new covenant as of the resurrection from the dead. In his famous vision of the dry bones in chapter 37 he pictures Israel as a corpse which will be revived only by the Spirit of God.

These prophets not only speak about marriage; through their own marriages (or lack thereof) they reflect God's marriage with Israel. Hosea exemplifies this well, for he is called to marry a prostitute in order that God's word may speak through him (Hosea 1:2). His prophetic message is communicated not only through prophetic oracles but through the word which is "incarnate" in him. Jeremiah does not explain his marital situation so clearly, but one may well suspect that the reason why God commands Jeremiah not to marry (Jeremiah 16:1) is that he is called to reflect through his celibacy the divorce of Israel and God. Unlike

Jeremiah, Ezekiel is happily married and thus initially does not seem to reflect the divine-human relation as Hosea and Jeremiah do. When his wife dies, however, he is commanded not to mourn for her in order that he may reflect God's lack of grief over the fall of Jerusalem (Ezekiel 24:15 ff.).

An explanation of just why the human marriage of the prophet should be used to reflect the covenantal situation of Israel must be left until we have looked with greater care at the theological understanding of marriage offered in Scripture.[18] It is sufficient here to point out that there does seem to be a direct relation between the divine-human covenant and human marriage, a relation which has profound implications for the biblical view of sex, love, and marriage.

Thus far we have reviewed several different metaphorical ways of viewing the covenant and hence understanding the place of the Ten Commandments. It is important to recognize that no one of these symbols had absolute priority in Israel; no one metaphor can express the meaning of the covenant in all its richness. It is for this reason that both in the Old Testament and in the New the metaphors are constantly being mixed together in a somewhat confusing way. Jesus, for instance, insofar as he is the word of God, is described as the king, the bridegroom, the master. As the embodiment of Israel he is pictured as the son, the servant, and the high priest. All of these images are drawn from the Old Testament and find their roots, in one way or another, in the Torah.

## "OUT OF THE LAND OF EGYPT"

Scripture never lets the reader forget for long that the faith of Israel is a historical faith. No sooner has the name of God been uttered than it is qualified—or better explicated—by the reminder that Yahweh is the God who has led Israel out of Egypt. Faith in the name is anchored and concretized by the remembrance of the good news: Yahweh has brought us out.

For Israel this is the incontrovertible, central memory which must not be forgotten. Still there are those who stand outside the

18. Infra, ch. 9.

circle of faith who ask questions which must be answered. Was there really a bondage at all? How long did it last? When did the bondage begin and when did it end? The faith of Israel does not, indeed cannot, rely on only extrabiblical sources, but it may be helpful to turn to such sources, as well as to the Bible, to answer these objective historical questions.

There was a time when some scholars called into question the whole idea of a period of bondage and argued that it was but a piece of fanciful fiction, but today there are few who would take such a radical position. It may be, some would argue, that not all the tribes experienced such bondage. Still, no nation as proud as Israel would have fabricated such a degrading tale. Ancient peoples invariably exulted in tracing their ancestry back to some great hero or demigod. Israel's admission—no, proclamation—that she was once enslaved in Egypt is self-authenticating from an anthropological point of view.

Just how long Israel was in Egypt, however, is a more difficult question. According to Abraham's vision in Genesis 15, which may, of course, have been written after the fact, Israel was to have been "oppressed" in Egypt for four hundred years. Since, according to Exodus, Israel was not oppressed during at least a portion of her sojourn there, this would make the actual stay in Egypt considerably longer than that.

Exodus 12:40, on the other hand, states: "The time that the people of Israel dwelt in Egypt was four hundred and thirty years." This period would apparently include both the years before a king arose who "knew not Joseph" and the many years of oppression, and therefore would be shorter than the time estimated in Genesis 15. The truncated genealogy in Exodus 6:14–25 complicates the matter still more, for it lists only four generations from Levi to Moses (Levi, Kohath, Amram, Moses). Although the given ages of the first three men add up to four hundred seven years, one can hardly argue that this figure can be reconciled with the figure given in Exodus 12:40, for obviously generations overlap.

Any attempt to solve this problem must, by necessity, be based on a large number of suppositions and hypotheses, but if one is willing to accept the implications of the probable, some rather general conclusions can be reached through which we can at least put the claims of the Bible in better historical perspective.

The best place to begin in discussing the time Israel spent in Egypt is with the terminal date for that sojourn. Although there has been great scholarly debate concerning this matter in the past, it appears that the majority of scholars now favors a date in the first half of the thirteenth century B.C. This conclusion is based upon several pieces of evidence. Most important, perhaps, is the fact that an invasion of Canaan—particularly of the southern hill country—took place in the late thirteenth century.[19] If one can believe, as many do, that these invasions were a part of the conquest described in Joshua, then the exodus must have taken place somewhat earlier, probably in the first decades of that same century.

This means that the Pharaoh who ruled Egypt at the time of the exodus was probably Rameses II, who reigned from ca. 1290–1224 B.C. This supposition is supported by the correlation of biblical and nonbiblical evidence concerning the cities of Pithom and Raamses mentioned in Exodus 1:11. John Bright writes:

> "We are told (Exodus 1:11) that Hebrews were forced to labor at the building of Pithom and Raamses. The former lies at Tell er-Retabeh, west of Lake Timsah in northeastern Egypt; the latter is none other than the ancient Hyksos capital of Avaris, rebuilt and again made the capital by Sethos I and Rameses II, and called by the latter the "House of Rameses."[20]

The added fact that these cities were reportedly rebuilt during the reigns of Sethos I and Rameses II by enslaved 'apiru not only

19. John Bright, *A History of Israel* (Philadelphia: Westminster Press, 1959), pp. 119–120. Cf. John Gray, *Archaeology and the Old Testament World* (New York: Harper and Row, 1962), pp. 94–96. Gray argues that the destruction of such cities as Lachish and Debir may not have been caused by the Israelites. Although he is correct that there is no absolute proof that Israel destroyed these cities, the correlation of the biblical account and archaeological evidence makes Bright's position quite probable.

20. From *A History of Israel*, by John Bright, p. 111. © W. L. Jenkins, The Westminster Press, MCMLIX. Used by permission.

helps to date the exodus. Since *'apiru* may be equivalent to "Hebrew," it also tends to confirm the fact that Israel was truly enslaved in Egypt and was forced to labor in the service of the Pharaoh.[21]

The question remains, however, when did Israel enter Egypt? Any answer given to this question must be, until more evidence is uncovered, of a hypothetical nature. Still, it seems reasonable that Israel may have entered Egypt sometime during the reign of the Hyksos. The Hyksos were people of northwest Semitic stock[22] who invaded Egypt as early as 1720 B.C. Since Egypt was in a state of internal decay, these invaders were successful in their conquest and by 1680 controlled most of Egypt. It was the Hyksos who originally built Avaris (Tanis) near the northeastern frontier. Because these Hyksos were Semites it is quite likely that a man such as Joseph might well have found favor in their eyes and risen to a position of power. It is also quite likely that when they were finally driven out, the descendants of Joseph might have been looked upon with great suspicion. This expulsion occurred sometime before 1550 B.C. when Avaris was finally taken by the indigenous Egyptians and the Hyksos invaders were forced to flee.[23]

During the reign of Haremhab (ca. 1340–1310 B.C.) the four hundredth anniversary of the founding of Avaris was celebrated. Rameses II later erected a stele there mentioning the original founding of the city when he reestablished his capital on that

21. Ibid., pp. 85–86, 111. See also Albright, *From the Stone Age to Christianity,* pp. 239–41. It seems probable that the Israelites were a part of a much larger group of people called the *Khapiru* or *'apiru.* Albright writes, "The meaning of the term *Apiru- Abiru,* later 'Ibri, "hebrew," has now been established; it meant something like "donkey-man, donkey driver, huckster, caravaneer." Originally it may have meant "dusty," with obvious reference to the dust raised by donkeys on a much-traveled road. As we know from a multitude of passages, extending over a millennium, from the late third millennium to the twelfth century B.C., the Apiru were as a rule stateless persons of varied ethnic stock, scattered from Elam to Egypt." William Foxwell Albright, *The Biblical Period* (New York: Harper and Row, 1963), p. 5.

22. Bright, *A History of Israel,* p. 54.

23. Ibid., p. 55. The date of the conquest of Avaris by Amosis I is much disputed. Many other scholars (for instance, Gardiner and Noth) would date the expulsion of the Hyksos somewhat earlier.

site.[24] Although we cannot be sure that the Israelites knew of this stele, Numbers 13:22 indicates that they did know something about the date of Avaris's inception. This text reads:

> They went up into the Negeb, and came to Hebron; and Ahiman, Sheshai, and Talmai, the descendants of Anak, were there. (Hebron was built seven years before Zoan in Egypt.)

Because Zoan is the biblical name for Avaris, it is clear that the author of this parenthetical interjection had some idea about the date of the founding of the Hyksos capital of Egypt. Since the city was founded about four hundred years before the exodus, this may account for the biblical tradition that Israel spent a little over four hundred years in Egypt.

There is no easy way, however, to reconcile this information with the genealogy of Moses in Exodus 6 which lists only four generations from Levi to the great Hebrew leader. Perhaps this genealogy points to the fact that not all of the ancestors of those who were later to become members of the house of Israel arrived in Egypt at the same time. It may be that the tribe of Levi, though racially related to the Joseph tribes, actually did not join them in Egypt until only a few generations before the exodus. All of this is a matter of speculation which only more nonbiblical evidence (which is at present unavailable) can illumine. Be that as it may, it does seem reasonable to say that some segments of Israel were in Egypt for a long time, perhaps for more than four hundred years, that they were enslaved, and that somehow they escaped from Egypt.

## "OUT OF THE HOUSE OF BONDAGE"

Whether Israel was in Egypt for four hundred years or only for four generations, the fact is that she was in bondage long enough to lose her identity as a people and to pass into oblivion. Many other peoples have met their end more abruptly than this.

---

24. Ibid., p. 111. The dates of Haremhab's reign are in dispute. Sir Alan Gardiner (*Egypt of the Pharaohs* [New York: Oxford University Press, 1966], p. 443) conjectures that he ruled from 1335–1308 B.C.

Yet Israel did not die. Her mystery is the mystery of the bush which Moses saw on the slopes of Horeb. She is burned and burned and burned again; yet she is not consumed. Millions of the sons of Israel may perish, but Israel lives on. This is one of the strange facts of history which cannot be denied; it is the great sign which the history of Israel bears.

Scripture recognizes that this ability to survive the house of bondage is not just a natural characteristic of the people of Israel. She does not survive because of her cunning, virtue, or religious genius. She survives, this text proclaims, because her God is a God who brings out. Yahweh, of course, does not protect her no matter what she does. Like an eagle teaching its young to fly, he carries his people aloft and then releases them to fly by themselves. Sometimes Israel, in trying her wings, comes close to disaster; she sins and accordingly suffers historical catastrophe. Nevertheless, when the end seems near, God hears her cry and brings her out from death. The God of Israel, then, is the God of resurrection.

Nor is the victory of Yahweh a world-denying victory such as that claimed by the Buddha or the Hindu mystics. Israel is released from Egyptian bondage, but not from the world. Yahweh's act of bringing out is an affirmation that in spite of the human bondage which seems to prevail in the world, life is meaningful and worth living. The salvation of Israel must not be confused with the salvation (*soteria*) of the mystery cults. Israel is not saved by promises of heaven and immortality or by the revelation of some divine *gnosis* which provides an escape from this-worldly existence. She is saved by the very concrete crossing of the Sea of Reeds and by the knowledge that the Power of powers is the God who brings her out.

Israel's salvation should not be regarded as a salvation from the secularity of existence for a more "religious" destiny. From one perspective, Israel's salvation can be seen as the freedom from human religion. In Egypt, Israel came to know quite concretely the tyranny of the gods. The Pharaoh, the king of Egypt, was the unity and expression of all the so-called divine powers which controlled the lives of Egyptians. The victory of Yahweh was the victory of the true Power of the universe over all these pseudogods. Israel was freed from the multiplicity of powers so that she might find the unity of life which allows men to live simply as men. Israel was freed so that she could regard the world and its powers simply as "the world" and no more. No longer need Israel kowtow to this power or that. She is free to celebrate the secularity of existence because God has brought her out.

Throughout the Law and the Prophets Israel is reminded of the value of human freedom. She is called to remember again and again her days of bondage, not because she enjoyed the bondage, but because of its horror. And she is reminded repeatedly that since she is free she must be careful not to inflict bondage upon others. Leviticus contains this characteristic sentence:

> When a stranger sojourns with you in your land, you shall not do him wrong. The stranger who sojourns with you shall be to you as the native among you, and you shall love him as yourself; for you were strangers in the land of Egypt: I am the LORD your God (Leviticus 19:33–34).

On this basis the Torah also commands just and merciful treatment of the poor and downtrodden, the widows and the fatherless. Remember, says the Torah, that you were once in their condition and God had mercy upon you. Go and do thou likewise.

When Amos in the eighth century proclaimed his message of judgment against Israel he emphasized, in his attack upon the moral and religious corruption of the people, nothing particularly new. His concern for the poor and needy, for the widows and orphans is to be found in every "strata" of the Torah. Rather than introducing a new message, Amos simply restates in particularly compelling ways the message of the prologue to the Decalogue. If Israel is to be true to her heritage, she must remember that Yahweh has brought her out of the house of bondage and, therefore, must help to alleviate the bondage of others. Only when she does this can Israel claim to be in truth "a kingdom of priests and a holy nation."

## Chapter 5

# NO OTHER GODS

"You shall have no other gods before me."

When God spoke to Israel at Sinai in the thunder, he spoke one *dabar*, one meaningful event. Man, however, cannot speak with the fullness embodied in God's word, for no human word can capture the many-splendored brilliance of God's *dabar*. Hence, when Israel attempted to articulate in human words the word of thunder, she spoke not one word but ten. The preamble or, as Jewish tradition would have it, the first commandment, reflects the *dabar* directly by describing the event and identifying the speaker. The words which follow are an attempt to express the real meaning of what Yahweh has spoken in the exodus. The preamble, then, is not just a pious introduction to some ancient social legislation; it is like a flower bud which opens, displaying overtly in the Ten Commandments what it had implicitly contained.

What the reformed tradition calls the first commandment adds nothing to the preamble but only expresses more clearly an aspect of its inner meaning. Essentially, this commandment simply underlines the exclusive nature of the I-Thou covenantal relationship already mentioned in verse two. The fact that Yahweh is Israel's God means not only that he has committed himself to this people but that Israel must commit herself to him absolutely—as a wife does to her husband. She must have no other gods before him. Although this meaning is clear and relatively straightforward, both the wording and the implications of the commandment are such that we cannot pass over it without considering several problems.

### THE FACE OF GOD

Translated literally this commandment might read: "There shall not be to you other gods before (or above or upon) my face." Why *'al-pani*, before my face? It must be recognized at the outset that for Israel and, to a lesser extent, for us a face is more than just a physical part of a man. Rather it is the revelation of the self with which one confronts another; it is one's "presence" among men. Therefore we describe a man who withdraws himself with humility or servility from true encounter as "self-effacing." We speak of the multitude of men who have lost themselves in anonymity and thus no longer confront as the "faceless masses." We tell a man who wishes to retreat from a difficult problem to "face up to the situation."

God also has a face, a presence among men, which is both physical and yet self-revealing. In experiencing the exodus and in hearing God's voice in the thunder Israel is confronted by God's face and learns, through knowing him, that now she can no longer fear, worship, or believe in other powers. Before his face, that is before those very concrete and observable events which led to Israel's freedom, she must affirm that he is the one and only God. Now she knows that the whole realm of creation is, at least potentially, the face of God. She sees that in every vital encounter in which "Thou" is said the face of God is present.

This means, in effect, that the traditional doctrine of the invisibility of God is quite unbiblical. The whole Bible is, in various ways, an affirmation that God does have a face and that he can be seen and known if man only has the capacity to see. The intentions of God are not just a matter of idle speculation, for he reveals himself in and through the world.

Although Israel sees God's face at Sinai and speaks his name in response, she also knows that even in his revelation, God remains hidden. Exodus 33 makes this paradoxical presentness and hiddenness of God clear. On the one hand it is said that: "The LORD used to speak to Moses face to face, as a man speaks to his friend" (Exodus 33:11). Still, when Moses asks to see God's face and to gain thereby the assurance that God will go with them, the Lord responds:

"I will make all my goodness pass before you, and will proclaim before you my name 'The LORD'; and I will be gracious to whom I will be gracious, and will show mercy on whom I will show mercy. But," he said, "you cannot see my face; for man shall not see me and live" (Exodus 33:19–20).

Documentary critics argue that this apparent inconsistency between verse 11 and verse 20 exists because the chapter is composite: verse 11 comes from one source, verse 20 from another.[1] This explanation, however, does not clarify why an editor would leave these two verses side by side.

Is it not possible that these two sentences are purposely juxtaposed? Might it not be that the text reads as it does because there is a sense in which Israel both sees and does not see the face of God? God does reveal himself; his goodness and mercy are repeatedly made evident to Israel. In the exodus God reveals his name, but Moses wants to know more; he wants assurance about the future; he wants God to "show him his ways" (Exodus 33:13). This is precisely what God will not do. Just as the face of man reveals and yet hides a man's self; so God remains hidden even in the midst of his revelation. His way, his plan for the future, remains hidden and Moses must be content to see only God's back as he goes before him.

---

1. Martin Noth, *Exodus, A Commentary* (Philadelphia: Westminster Press, 1962), p. 258.

## MONOTHEISM OR HENOTHEISM

For many centuries this first commandment was understood as teaching the doctrine of monotheism, that is, that God is the only metaphysically real divine Being. In recent years, however, many scholars have raised objection to this interpretation by pointing out that the commandment does not deny the existence of other gods at all, but only commands Israel not to "have them."[2] Therefore, they describe the attitude of Israel, particularly during preexilic days as henotheistic—Israel recognized the reality of many gods but worshipped only one.

There are several indications that this latter interpretation may be correct. For instance, in a message to the king of the Ammonites, Jephthah writes: "Will you not possess what Chemosh your god gives you to possess? And all that the LORD our God has dispossessed before us, we will possess" (Judges 11:24).

This assertion should not be disturbing to those who have followed our argument thus far. In chapter two it was argued that the pagan gods and goddesses were, and indeed are, real "Powers," for they are the forces which do control the lives of men. The people of Israel recognized this fact and acknowledged that they were not just fiction. Since Chemosh was simply the personification of the power of the Ammonites, he was regarded as "real," as he who gave to the Ammonites what they possessed. Israel also knew, however, that the reality of these foreign gods was only a quasi-reality, an illusion to be dispelled. Though the goi'im worshipped these worldly powers, Israel knew that their worship was a delusion. She might speak of other gods as existent, but she also recognized that Yahweh alone controls the world and its powers.

This view of the gods may account for the peculiar nature of the biblical attack upon paganism which has been so clearly

2. Theophile James Meek, *Hebrew Origins* (New York: Harper and Brothers, 1950), p. 206 ff. Meek distinguishes between henotheism and monolatry. Essentially what he means by monolatry is what I choose to call henotheism.

analyzed by Yezekiel Kauffmann.[3] Kauffmann is quite right in observing that the biblical writers do not normally concern themselves with the existence or nonexistence of other gods or with the falsity of the pagan myths. What they attack is the making and worship of idols. Doubtless they approach the subject in this way because they do not wish to quarrel with either the reality of these powers or with the myths as accurate descriptions of their control over man's life. What they do deny categorically is that these gods should be worshipped and idolized.

The people of Israel, therefore, were neither monotheists (in the eighteenth century, rationalistic sense) nor henotheists (in the modern, anthropological sense). That is to say, they neither ascribed to an intellectualized belief in one God who, as a divine being, exists "somewhere" nor did they choose just one god from among the many to be theirs. Instead at Sinai they covenanted with the one all-embracing Power who causes all to come to pass and who has committed himself to Israel. The universality of the Deity is expressed by the word *'Elohim.* His particular relation to Israel is signified by the name Yahweh. Thus the most characteristic way of speaking of him is as *Yahweh 'Elohenu,* as the Lord our God.

The first commandment, then, is an affirmation of both the uniqueness of Israel and the unity of all existence and human life. It is an invitation, indeed a challenge, to see all aspects of life as integral parts of one common universe. God is not just the power of love, mercy, and peace. It is he who caused the catastrophic flood which only Noah survived, who causes the mountains to tremble and the heavens to withhold their rain. No power can be set over against Yahweh. For the believer in *Yahweh 'Elohenu* there can be no devils or demons, not even little ones.

## THE PROBLEM OF EVIL

This vision of a totally unified universe in which there are no forces apart from the Almighty raises in a most radical way

3. Yezekiel Kauffman, *The Religion of Israel,* translated and abridged by Moshe Greenberg (Chicago: University of Chicago Press, 1960), p. 7 ff.

the whole question of the reality of evil. If God is the totality of forces in the universe, is he not, in a direct sense, the cause of evil? This is certainly no unimportant or superfluous difficulty which can be dismissed with the remark that this is the best of all possible worlds. Nicholas Berdyaev is quite right in pointing to the problem of evil as *the* central problem which theologians disregard only at their own peril.[4]

It must be recognized at the outset that the biblical answer to the problem of evil is paradoxical. On the one hand, Scripture states over and over again that God is the cause of both good and what men call evil. God hardens Pharaoh's heart; he brings the plagues; he smites and kills with devastating fury. Amos sums up this side of the paradox in his famous question, "Does evil befall a city, unless the LORD has done it?" (Amos 3:6). On the other hand, Scripture also invariably recognizes that man is a moral being, that he makes choices, and that he is to be judged guilty or innocent upon the basis of these choices. Amos may believe that God is wholly in charge and that it is he who brings the invading armies against Israel, but he also believes that Israel (and Assyria) is morally responsible and brings punishment upon itself.

The question is: How can one claim that God is Almighty and yet believe that man is a moral agent who makes real choices of his own? The fact of the matter is that Scripture does not try to resolve this difficulty. What appears to us as a problem is presented simply as the truth of life, as a paradoxical fact of existence. Pain, suffering, cruelty, and oppression are real. They cannot be willed away by the pious phrase that the world belongs to God and, therefore, whatever is is right. Israel is called to "seek justice, correct oppression; defend the fatherless, plead for the widow" (Isaiah 1:17). Nevertheless, Paul's affirmation that "in everything God works for good with those who love him" (Romans 8:28) expresses equally well the other side of Israel's

4. Nicolai Berdyaev, *The Destiny of Man,* trans. Natalie Duddington (New York: Harper and Row, 1960), chap. 2.

view of life. Israel is called both to work for justice that the world may conform to the will of God and to accept the events which occur as an expression of that same will.

Although the Bible, in general, affirms this paradox repeatedly, the story of Adam, as it is presented in Genesis 2 and 3, has often been taken as an attempt to resolve it. That is, it has been interpreted as an explanation of why man is "sinful," and why, therefore, there is evil in the universe. Nothing could be further from the truth, for, far from resolving the paradox, the story of Adam only accentuates it.

The first point to be made about the story of Adam is that it is not just a historical account of our primordial ancestor. *'Adam* means simply "man." Nevertheless, man as he exists is always an individual living in a particular time and in a particular place. Hence, the story is set at a specific time in Eden. Although Eden is a specific place, it is also said to be the source of all human culture, for out of the garden flows a river which divides into the Pishon (probably the Indus), the Gihon (the Nile), the Hiddekel (the Tigris), and the Euphrates.[5] Eden is, then, the source for the great human civilizations; Adam is the father of civilized man as he exists in historical times. He is an individual; yet his story is meant to be a mirror for all men.

According to the first chapter of Genesis both the world and man are created by God and are pronounced "good" *(tob)*.[6] There is no principle of evil or demonic force standing over against God, warring with him. Nor is there any hint that the second account of creation in Genesis 2–3 takes a different point of view. Adam, as created by God, is the highest and noblest of

5. It seems to me that any attempt (such as is found in Emil G. Kraeling, *Bible Atlas* [New York: Rand McNally and Co., 1966], p. 42) to interpret Genesis 2 as a literal picture of how Israel thought about the world geographically is doomed to failure. I doubt very much that the Israelites, who knew quite well where the Tigris and Euphrates began, ever thought of the Nile, Tigris, Euphrates, and Indus rivers as flowing from the same source. This detail of the story shows that the Israelites knew that they were speaking mythologically in this chapter of Genesis.

6. The word *tob* which is used in Genesis 1 can be given ethical connotations but means first of all "sweet-smelling."

105

God's creatures and is given dominion over the earth. Paradoxically, however, man and woman disobey God and follow the advice of the serpent. They eat of the tree of the knowledge of good and evil and soon learn the meaning of guilt and shame. Sin is not specifically mentioned until Genesis 4:7 and thus it may be inappropriate to call the story of Genesis 3 the story of man's fall into sin. Still, this act of disobedience is seen as the root of sin and of the consequent disorders which plague the world.

A number of questions must be asked. First, is the serpent meant to represent some preexistent demonic power? Genesis itself answers this question by describing the serpent as "more subtle than any other wild creature that the LORD God had made" (Genesis 3:1). The serpent may be the locus for temptation, but is not evil incarnate. At most, the serpent represents the possibility of man's disobedience.[7] This mysterious creature, whom many ancient men thought was immortal,[8] had the capacity to awake in Adam a sense of discontentedness and a desire to transcend the bounds of his finitude. Essentially, however, it was not the serpent, but man's capacity to be dissatisfied with his own created condition which produced disobedience.

Second, we must ask, why was the fruit of the tree of the knowledge of good and evil forbidden man? Why did God, who consistently exhorts Israel to do righteousness and avoid evil, not want Adam to know good and evil? Many different answers have been given to this question. The interpretation which commends itself most to me is this: If God created the world good, there cannot, by definition, be any true possibility of distinguishing good and evil. To pronounce anything evil is to set oneself up as a judge of God and all that he has done. The serpent, itself a good creation, awakens in the woman a sense of dread and anxiety. This dread is the beginning of woman's (and, of course, man's) downfall, for when they begin to say "this creature is 'evil,'" they place themselves as judges over God.

---

7. Søren Kierkegaard, *The Concept of Dread,* trans. Walter Lowrie (Princeton, N.J.: Princeton University Press, 1944), pp. 38–39.
8. Thorkild Jacobsen, "Mesopotamia," in *Before Philosophy,* ed. H. Frankfort et al. (London: Penguin Books, 1954), p. 227.

The results of this "value judgment" are far-reaching. When the man and woman begin to judge creation, they immediately see their own genitals and are repulsed by them. The woman, who was taken out of man and thus is dependent upon him and whose natural biological function is to desire her husband and bear children, now finds her glory a painful curse (Genesis 3:16). The man, who is made to till the garden and keep it, regards his labor as a burden and hates the weeds which grow among his crops (Genesis 3:17). He also finds that the woman, whom he had gladly proclaimed to be "bone of his bone and flesh of his flesh," is the source of his discontent. Both man and woman, as a result of their newly acquired "knowledge," look upon their mortality, their finite humanness, with aversion and desire what was never really theirs, immortality (Genesis 3:19).

In Genesis, therefore, the root of evil is found in man's own unique propensity to transcend and consequently to judge the world in which he lives. Creation, despite the rule of fang and claw, is pronounced good by God. When man judges certain aspects of it evil, he finds himself alienated from his wife, the land, and God. Because Adam finds himself so alienated, he attempts to free himself from what he regards as his curse and hence falls deeper and deeper into sin. The question of "natural evil" therefore becomes itself the root of the more horrible evil, human depravity.

There is no implication, however, that man can give up this propensity to judge creation. Once the Rubicon is crossed and man awakes from his dreaming innocence to judge his environment, there is no retreat.[9] The more man tries to return to his "natural state," the more intense the shame tends to become. God recognizes this and therefore clothes the man and woman in

9. Only in the book of Ecclesiastes does there seem to be an attempt to avoid the distinctions of good and evil. Koheleth sees that man's ability to transcend himself leads inevitably to the attitude, "Vanity of vanities, all is vanity." Hence, he counsels man to accept the world as it is, without placing value judgments upon the time of pain and sorrow. I doubt, however, whether many can really follow Koheleth's wisdom when the times of weeping come.

animal skins himself (Genesis 3:21). He may punish man dreadfully for his "evil imagination," but God also recognizes that "the imagination of man is evil from his youth" (Genesis 8:21) and offers him, as a consequence, a covenant of hope.

Nor is the "fall" itself regarded as wholly "evil." Before the act of disobedience, Adam may have lived in a blissful and innocent harmony with creation and his Creator; yet only man outside of Eden builds human society and culture. The Gihon, Pishon, Hiddekel, and Euphrates flow outside of the garden. Cain's children are the inventors of music, metalworking, and the like; the wages of sin are the price man pays for his high cultural and intellectual achievements.

Genesis does not try to answer the question of why God allowed man to become so alienated. To justify God's ways to man is but another way of attempting to stand in judgment over God and this Genesis will not do. Genesis will describe man's alienated condition, but will not and cannot say why this inevitable condition exists. So we are left where we began, with a paradox. Man is guilty; he has falsely judged creation and so has brought his condition of insecurity upon himself; yet why God created man with the capacity so to judge, and why man inevitably follows this course of judgment is left unexplained. The most that can be said is that man would not be man—he could not dominate the earth—without the ability to transcend himself.

To point out the inconsistency of this position is, of course, quite simple. Every schoolboy knows that there is something logically wrong with the assertion that man is both finite and free. Nevertheless, it is far easier to criticize this paradox than to work out a convincing, nonparadoxical alternative. In truth, the Bible wrestles, as we all must, with the fact that man's existence is paradoxical. Looked at from the point of view of his finitude, man appears unfree, but looked at from the point of view of his freedom man appears infinite; yet both man's finitude and his freedom must be affirmed if one is to describe adequately the mystery which is man. When man is examined "objectively," as something in the "phenomenal world" to be studied, man's freedom seems to evaporate and he appears as the product of conditioning. When man looks at himself "subjectively" he knows the reality of choice and hence must regard himself as free and morally responsible. Since man knows himself in both ways, it is impossible to disregard either his finitude or his freedom without destroying the essence of man as he is known. Man must live in this paradox.

The biblical writers sense most deeply this paradoxical position of man as he stands before God. Martin Buber expresses this view well when he writes:

> But if I consider necessity and freedom not in worlds of thought but in the reality of my standing before God, if I know that 'I am given over for disposal' and know at the same time that 'It depends on myself,' then I cannot try to escape the paradox that has to be lived by assigning the irreconcilable propositions to two separate realms of validity; nor can I be helped to an ideal reconciliation by any theological device: but I am compelled to take both myself, to be lived together, and in being lived they are one.[10]

This is, in truth, the attitude of the Bible from beginning to end.

In the second chapter of our study we discussed briefly the metaphor of creation which pictures God as a poet who creates the universe and history "out of nothing" by speaking his word. Such a picture is, of course, poetical and not descriptive in any literal or positivistic sense. Since we can only speak figuratively of creation, however, it may provide a clue to the understanding of the problem of evil. God, the artist, has created man with freedom of choice. This he gives to man by giving him a commandment which he can disobey. Once God has done this, he must allow for disobedience and hence for sin. God could, of course, destroy sin and evil, but he cannot do so without violating the integrity of his characters. Sin cannot be destroyed in fact without eliminating the man whom he has created. Man could not be man;

10. Martin Buber, *I and Thou,* trans. Ronald Gregor Smith (New York: Charles Scribner's Sons, 1958), p. 96. Used by permission.

he could not dominate the earth and subdue it without freedom of choice. Hence God continues to create man, the sinner, even though the sin violates his will for man; yet out of the sin itself he also brings good. Sin is punished by sin itself. God will not simply overlook it, but he also turns man's sin to good. Even Judas's act of betrayal must be described as "O felix culpa."

## THE SECULAR AND THE SACRED

One of the characteristic impulses of modern culture is the repeated attempt to distinguish and separate the secular and the sacred, the worldly and the religious, the church and the state. "Render therefore to Caesar the things that are Caesar's, and to God the things that are God's" (Matthew 22:21)—this is the proof text of modern culture and many take pride in having discovered such a neat answer to age-old questions. After centuries of conflict between the proponents of an ecclesiocracy and the proponents of caesaropapism, the modern world has settled upon a truce which accords to state and church alike a sphere of influence. The state is in charge of temporal affairs, while the church deals with spiritual matters.

Seen from one perspective, this separation which so profoundly affects our whole culture has sound biblical precedent. The men of Israel were usually, if not always, careful to distinguish between the will of God and the will of the king and thus criticized rulers who sought to assume priestly authority.[11] Furthermore, the true prophet was never a domesticated servant of the royal house. He came, it seemed, from out of nowhere to speak his message of judgment against the Establishment. The word of God, as spoken by the prophets, was, more often than not, a word directed against the actions of the king and his administration. One of the most distinctive features of Israel's religion was, in fact, the distinction made between the will of Yahweh and the nation's self-interest.

11. See, for instance, 2 Chronicles 26:16–21.

This does not mean, however, that the modern distinction between the secular and the sacred is wholly biblical. Although the Law and the Prophets teach that the will of God cannot be identified with the will of men, they also teach that his will cannot be separated from any sphere of life. Israel can recognize no power beside the power of Yahweh. God is not just the overseer of cultic acts or the giver of fleeting feelings of peace to the soul. He is the ruler of all life; there can be for Israel no other power beside him.

To affirm the first commandment means two seemingly contradictory things: First, it means that all the various powers of the universe—both the physical and the social—are God-given; they are manifestations of his will. Whatever happens, happens according to his purposes. Second, and conversely, it also means that the use of all of these various powers is subject to God and thus stands under his judgment. Here we return to the central paradox of free will and determinism already discussed. The biblical attitude is, because of this paradox, both conservative and revolutionary at the same time. Scripture proclaims the state to be ordained by God; yet the prophets call down God's judgment upon the state as it exists. This is not just an inconsistency among authors. It is a paradox which lies at the heart of the biblical message. To all the powers of existence the believer must utter both a "Yes" and a "No."

Because in recent years many believers have tended to confuse the separation of church and state with the separation of God and the secular world, it is not surprising that in our own time there has been a needed reaction to this aberration. Today the theological watchword is "secular." Although Dietrich Bonhoeffer would undoubtedly criticize many of his would-be followers, he initiated, or at least eloquently fostered, a movement away from a faith concerned with cultic religion to a faith concerned with the secular world. Harvey Cox represents at least one side of this movement through his book, *The Secular City,* in which he argues against a Christianity concerned primarily with the cult and for a faith which accepts and is involved in the things of this world. His image of the church as being like a "floating crap game" which goes where the action is, sums up his attitude.[12]

As important as Cox's work is in clearing the air about a number of important issues, he fails to take into account the full content of the "Exodus faith" which he claims to affirm. Israel, at her best, never identified the service of her God with merely cultic activities. The God of Israel is the God of this world and not just of religion. But God is still the God of the cult. Throughout the Bible, even in the works of the prophets, the cult and religion are given their due. Although cultic acts do not comprise the whole of obedience to God, they are an important part of it, for they remind Israel of her past and those events through which God spoke. Without the cult, Israel would have quickly forgotten her *raison d'être* and would have soon fallen again into a new form of Egyptian bondage. The cult is not an end in itself, as it has become for many modern-day Christians. Without the preaching, teaching, and worship of religion, however, the people of God would soon develop a kind of amnesia and loss of self-identity. The perspective of Sinai would be lost and thus the true meaning of secularity would be forgotten as well. Cox speaks cogently about the relevance of the gospel for the world; his word is one which the church badly needs, but in *The Secular City* he seemed to forget that men of faith are still finite, sinful men who need reminders of things past and symbolic ways of expressing their faith in the present if they are to be truly secular.

Cox is also correct in pointing out that there is a sense in which the church should stop lamenting the fact that the world has become secular. If history is in the hands of God, then we should accept the secularization of the West as a manifestation of his will. Cox fails to see, however, that such acceptance must also be qualified by a paradoxical "No." Secularization may be an inevitable development, but it also stands under the judgment of God.

12. Harvey Cox, *The Secular City: Secularization and Urbanization in Theological Perspective* (New York: Macmillan Co., 1965), p. 125.

The believer's attitude toward the secular world, when guided by the first commandment, therefore, is paradoxical. He must accept the developments of history and culture as somehow a manifestation of God's will; yet he must also recognize that God stands in judgment over the injustices and idolatries perpetrated by men. He must resist all attempts to subordinate state to church; yet he must also proclaim and work for the Lordship of God in the world. He must defend the importance of religion; yet he must remain ever critical of the arrogance and irrelevance of the cult. The first commandment teaches that the world is both entirely secular and entirely sacred. It is a vale of tears in which injustice and sin prevail; yet it is also the good earth, created and sustained by the good Creator who causes to pass what comes to pass.

## Chapter 6

# IDOLS AND IMAGES

You shall not make yourself a graven image, or any likeness of anything that is in heaven above, or that is in the earth beneath, or that is in the water under the earth; you shall not bow down to them or serve them; for I the LORD your God am a jealous God, visiting the iniquity of the fathers upon the children to the third and the fourth generation of those who hate me, but showing steadfast love to thousands of those who love me and keep my commandments (Exodus 20:4–6).

Israel was admonished by the first commandment to turn from the worship of the finite powers of this life to the service of the ultimate source of these powers, Yahweh. The second commandment not only confirms this prohibition but adds something very significant, indeed very startling, about the worship of the one true 'Elohim whose name is Yahweh. It proclaims that he must be worshipped without images, without any likeness being made of him, that he must not be represented by anything in the universe. While the first commandment limits Israel's worship to Yahweh, the second circumscribes decisively the way in which Yahweh must be worshipped. Thus, although these two commandments belong together, it is appropriate to treat them as two rather than one.

In order to understand the true import of this second commandment, one must first comprehend something of the importance of idols for the religions of ancient men. For the pagan peoples, who worshipped the various finite powers of existence, idols were an essential part of life. Although these polytheists surely did not quite believe, as Deutero-Isaiah implies,[1] that a piece of wood or metal was itself the god worshipped, they did regard their idols as objects through which communication with the deities could take place.

The polytheists recognized that man's life is affected profoundly by the cosmic, social, and subconscious powers of existence. Confronted directly, these powers appear as seemingly uncontrollable and hence frightening urgings and forces which drive men aimlessly, as the wind and waves batter a small boat at sea. The making of images not only expressed in a visual way the reality of these powers; it also provided, through objectification, a means whereby a person could deal with them. The idols of ancient men were a way of putting existence in order and hence of achieving sanity. By creating idols and images of the deities, men could place these forces at "arm's length" so that they could be addressed and placated. Idols, then, are an expression of a conviction that though men are motivated by the powers, men can also transcend them. They not only express the reality of the powers represented; they also covertly express the reality and independence of the human ego.[2] Through this objectification ancient man thought himself able to chart his own course upon the sea of subconscious, social, and cosmic powers which surrounded him.

1. Isaiah 40:18–20, 41:7, 44:9–20.
2. If one wished to use Freudian terminology, one could say that the making of idols is an attempt to protect the ego from the forces of the id and superego. Through the process of objectification, the ego attempts to express and yet put in their proper place the interior and exterior forces that threaten continually the ego's well-being.

The word spoken to Israel at Sinai, however, denies the possibility of this objectification of the deity. In the exodus Yahweh revealed himself to be far more than one power among many. Through his act of manumission he showed himself to be the Lord of all the powers of creation. The Nile turned red, the sun was darkened, the locusts swarmed, the wind blew at his command. In all these events, he revealed himself to be *Yahweh 'Elohim,* the ruler of all the powers of existence.

Each of these powers, by itself, can be described, defined, and imagined, for each is finite. Hence, it was quite appropriate for the pagans, who thought of these as separate powers, to describe them through the making of images and other likenesses. Yahweh, however, is not finite; he is not limited in any way. He is all power, all might. How then can he be described, imagined, or defined? A definition, by its very nature, implies that its object can be distinguished from other objects, that the object is limited in certain ways, it is one among many. But Yahweh is unlimited; he is *'Elohim.* To define him is to transform him into a limited being who is not truly almighty.

Since the second commandment is primarily an attempt to assert the indefinability and incomprehensibility of God in the face of humanity's natural propensity to make idols, it is far more universal in scope than at first meets the eye. Not only are the carved and molded images of the polytheist forbidden, Israel is also commanded not to make any *temunah,* any form, image, or likeness of her God, for God is beyond any limiting picture or description. Thus the commandment applies just as rigorously to the theologian who makes lofty definitions which claim to delineate God's essence as to the wood-carver or metalworker.

The second commandment, therefore, deals not only with some details of ancient worship and cultic practice which are primarily of antiquarian interest. It teaches the indefinability of God. It reminds Israel ever again that her "God is too small," that her comprehension of the Almighty is limited to her own human perspectives, and that man must never equate any human words

or ideas with the complete truth about him. This commandment
is a call to intellectual humility and repentance on the part of the
believer—particularly on the part of the theologian. It is a
reminder that human conceptions, even biblical conceptions, are
finite, limited, and wanting.

Thus this second word is the basis for all theological demythologizing. In its light no "myth" about God, be it the first chapter
of Genesis or the last chapter of John's Gospel, can be taken as
an adequate description of the reality considered. The theologian
is called to be vigilant in his attempts to distinguish between the
myths about God and God himself. The second commandment,
however, goes far beyond the position maintained by most modern
demythologizers. Although Bultmann at his best knows better, he
sometimes writes as though he believes that if we simply strip
away the now outmoded bits of ancient cosmology and mythology
by translating them into existentialist language we can arrive at
clear, descriptive statements about God, man, and the universe.[3]
This, according to the second commandment, is an illusion. We
may have to write new myths and make new metaphors in the
twentieth century in order to make the meaning of the Bible clear,
but we cannot do away with myths if we wish to say anything
at all about God.

Israel has not been alone in seeing that God is ultimately
indefinable and incomprehensible. Many philosophers and mystics
from both the East and the West have come to a similar conclusion. Plotinus, for instance, believed that nothing true can be said
positively about the One, for the One is beyond all human comprehension. Men can have a mystical "vision" of the One, but
this experience is ineffable. Hence Plotinus claimed that it is
impossible to say anything positive about the source of reality.

That Israel did not arrive at the same conclusion is clearly
illustrated by verse five. In fact, this verse follows verse four as

3. For instance, Bultmann writes, "When we speak of God as acting, we
do not speak mythologically in an objectifying sense." *Jesus Christ and
Mythology* (New York: Charles Scribner's Sons, 1958), p. 62.

something of a shock. After teaching the indescribability of God the commandment continues:

> For I the LORD your God am a jealous God, visiting the iniquity of the fathers upon the children to the third and the fourth generation of those who hate me, but showing steadfast love to thousands of those who love me and keep my commandments
>
> (Exodus 20:5–6).

How inconsistent this appears! After the commandment that no likeness of God be made from upon the earth, God is described very clearly as being like a jealous husband who will not abide unfaithfulness. How can verses four and five be reconciled?

Unlike Plotinus and the other mystics who have come to "God" through contemplation of "being," Israel was confronted by her God through the events of her life. As a result, although she knew and understood in depth his incomprehensibility, she also felt herself compelled to proclaim his reality and to exult in his presence. After crossing the Reed Sea, Miriam could not say with dispassionate objectivity, "God is incomprehensible; therefore, I will say nothing." No, she was compelled by the event to dance and burst into songs of praise: "Sing to the LORD, for he has triumphed gloriously; the horse and his rider he has thrown into the sea" (Exodus 15:21). Furthermore, Israel knew that it is just as incorrect to say that God is impersonal as it is to say that he is personal. Plotinus, in his attempt to avoid describing God, really turned God into a kind of "divine light bulb." This Israel would not do and therefore chose another path, using the most shocking anthropomorphisms and anthropopathisms to speak of God. The incomprehensible fire of existence is described as jealous, loving, and wrathful. To him Israel says, "Our King, Our Husband, Our Father." This is the tension in which Israel lives: she cannot speak of God; yet she must speak of God. She must demythologize and mythologize all at once.

This problem of religious language constitutes an ever-present quandary for the faithful. What is important, however, is not to solve the problem, for it is unresolvable, but to recognize its inevitability. The literalist fails to see the inadequacy of human language to say anything about God and thus turns the Bible into an idol. The demythologizer, though he rightly attacks the literalist, all too often makes the same mistake. Many modern theologians resort to the language of existentialism or classical ontology, as though the terms "being" and "becoming" are more exact than "Father" or "Husband." This second commandment, on the contrary, teaches that we must live with our "broken myths." Since we must speak of God but cannot speak accurately, we must use mythological language, the language of metaphor and simile, recognizing all the time that the words of men are finite and fallible and finally inadequate for the task.

## RELIGIOUS LANGUAGE AND THE IMAGE OF GOD

If we must use metaphors and analogies to speak of God, what type of metaphor is most appropriate? Why does the second commandment, indeed, the whole Bible, speak of God in anthropomorphic terms? The answer to this question—or at least a clue to the answer—is found in the first chapter of Genesis.

> Then God said, "Let us make man in our image, after our likeness; and let them have dominion over the fish of the sea, and over the birds of the air, and over the cattle, and over all the earth, and over every creeping thing that creeps upon the earth." So God created man in his own image, in the image of God he created him; male and female he created them (Genesis 1:26–27).

The second commandment forbids Israel to make any *pesel* or *temunah* of God. Man cannot make or imagine an image of his Creator—but God has done so. In fact, he has created man himself in his own image. Whether the *pesel* and *temunah* of Exodus 20:4 are meant to call to mind the *selem* and *damut* (the image and likeness) of Genesis 1:26 is not certain. The documentary critic would doubtless say no, for the sources are different. Nevertheless, the parallel is striking. The subtlety with which the pattern is repeated but the meaning changed may be accidental, but it surely is an arresting coincidence. *Pesel* and *temunah* obviously represent man-made fakes; *selem* and *damut* are authentic. Man cannot create images of God; he must be satisfied with and rejoice in the fact that he *is* that image.

There has been much debate throughout the centuries concerning just what is meant when it is said that man is made in the image of God. The exegete cannot avoid this difficult and highly significant theological question, for the answer to it affects the interpretation of the whole biblical message. Therefore, it is extraordinarily important that the text be examined carefully. Perhaps the best way to begin is negatively. Although a positive interpretation is difficult to make, clearly Genesis 1:26 does *not* mean, for instance, that man has a "spark of divinity" within him, some hidden godliness which needs only to be nurtured and developed in order for man to achieve deification. The Bible makes clear repeatedly that man is created from the dust of the earth. He is *basar*, flesh. Man may be above the beasts, for he is their ruler; yet he shares with them creatureliness and finitude. The higher animals, in fact, are said to have been created along with man on the sixth day. The clear implication is that although man may be the highest form of animal life, he is still an animal.

Nor does the Old Testament teach that the image of God is to be found in man's immortal soul. To be sure, God breathes into man the breath of life so that he becomes a "living soul," but this soul is not the immortal substance of Plato's *Phaedo* which flies to the world of forms after death.[4] For the Hebrew the soul, the *nepeš*, is just the principle of life, that which distinguishes the animate from the inanimate.

If, then, there is nothing about man's body or soul which is metaphysically like God, what does it mean to say that man is made in the image of God? It should be observed at the outset that the Bible does not claim to know anything about the meta-

---

4. H. Wheeler Robinson, *Inspiration and Revelation in the Old Testament* (Oxford: Clarendon Press, 1962), p. 70.

physical makeup of God. We do not, we cannot know what God is in himself. All that we can know about God is what he does, how he "is to us." Man is said to be made in the image of God, not because his psychic structure is trinitarian or even because he is a "rational" being, but because his actions mirror the actions of God.

This interpretation is clearly borne out by Genesis itself. The text reads: "Let us make man in our image . . . and let them have dominion . . ." (Genesis 1:26). In other words, man reflects God's dominion over creation by his own dominion over the earth. Man is God's vice-regent and as such he reflects God's action through his own. Man's ability to have dominion, of course, springs from certain human capacities, perhaps, as Reinhold Niebuhr would have it, from the capacity of man to transcend himself.[5] The Bible, however, does not attempt to define or describe such capacities, for they are ultimately an indescribable mystery. The most that Genesis will do is to point to man's dominion over creation and say, that is like God.

Man's ability to dominate is only one aspect of God's reflection in man. Genesis also seems to point to man's act of entering into community as male and female to procreate as a reflection of God's creation. This, at least, may be the meaning behind the strange way in which God speaks of himself both as singular and plural.

> Then God said, "Let us make man in our image, after our likeness; . . ." So God created man in his own image, in the image of God he created him; male and female he created them
> (Genesis 1:26, 27).

We shall explore the meaning of this passage more fully in chapter eight. Perhaps it suffices here to say that in some way, the duality of male and female in 'adam is seen to reflect a duality in the heart of God himself.

5. Reinhold Niebuhr, *The Nature and Destiny of Man* (New York: Charles Scribners' Sons, 1953), vol. 1, pp. 13–14.

In any event, the fact that man is made in God's image serves as a key for understanding how man can speak of God. Although Israel is not allowed to make an image of God, she can point to the image which God has made and thus illumine what she means by the name *Yahweh 'Elohenu.* In this second commandment Israel turns to the image of God as it is reflected in human relations between a man and his wife. Do you wish to understand how God will treat Israel? Then consider, says the commandment, how a good husband, who is jealous of his wife's affections, will treat her.

## COVENANTAL LOVE

For I the LORD your God am a jealous God, visiting the iniquity of the fathers upon the children to the third and the fourth generation of those who hate me, but showing steadfast love to thousands of those who love me and keep my commandments (Exodus 20:5).

This justification and warning which is appended to the second commandment begins with a threat and ends with a promise. From a hortatory point of view this order is correct. To understand the nature of the covenant as it was meant to be kept, however, it may be fruitful to begin with the second half of the justification. Only in the light of the true meaning of the covenant can its corruptions be fully understood.

One of the distinctive features of this commandment is the contrast which is drawn between the attitude demanded by the pagan gods and that required by the Lord of Israel. Israel is commanded not to make *pesel* or *temunah* nor to bow down to them *(tištahveh)* nor serve them *(ta 'abdem).* These words not only express cultic acts; they imply a kind of servility associated with slavery. Yahweh, in contrast, demands not the obedience of bondage but the obedience of love *('ahabah).*

Much has been made in recent years, not only by Anders Nygren but by others as well, concerning the distinction between the two Greek words for love, *agape* and *eros*.[6] In fact, many theologians have based their understanding of the biblical doctrine of love almost exclusively upon the distinction between these two words. *Eros,* it is said, is a grasping kind of love which seeks its own ends. *Agape,* on the other hand, is overflowing, self-giving love. *Eros* is the acquisitive love of sinful man. *Agape* is the love of God for man, a love which gives freely and bountifully. It is not a love which possesses but a love which "empties itself."

This is, to be sure, an accurate way of distinguishing these two Greek words; it is a distinction which teaches us something about the biblical doctrine of love. Unfortunately, however, many theologians have depended solely upon this Greek distinction without recognizing that in general the New Testament, though written in Greek, is governed from beginning to end by Hebraic ways of thinking. Moreover, although the Hebrew does not entirely destroy this *agape-eros* distinction, it does modify it considerably. If we are to understand fully the biblical understanding of love we must examine not only *eros* and *agape* but *'ahabah* and *hesed* as well.

The word *'ahabah* (verb: *'ahab*) which is used here to refer to the love which Yahweh demands of Israel is strikingly erotic in its connotations. It means, for instance, "to desire, to breathe after, to love, to delight in."[7] Although employed in a variety of ways, it is the word most often used to describe a woman's love for a man. Yahweh says, in effect, that he wants his people to love him in the way that the dark and comely girl loves her shepherd lad in the Song of Songs.

> As an apple tree among the trees of the wood,
>   so is my beloved among young men.
> With great delight I sat in his shadow,

6. Anders Nygren, *Agape and Eros,* trans. Philip S. Watson (Philadelphia: Westminster Press, 1953), passim. Karl Barth, *Church Dogmatics. A Selection,* trans. G. W. Bromiley (New York: Harper and Row, 1961), pp. 173–193.

7. *Gesenius' Hebrew and Chaldee Lexicon to the Old Testament Scriptures,* ed. Samuel Prideaux Tregelles (Grand Rapids, Mich.: Wm. B. Eerdmans, 1954), pp. 15–16.

and his fruit was sweet to my taste.
He brought me to the banqueting house,
 and his banner over me was love.
Sustain me with raisins, refresh me with apples;
 for I am sick with love

(Song of Songs 2:3–5).

The word for love used throughout this passage is *'aḫabah*, the love demanded of Israel by Yahweh in the second commandment. Further significance is added to this passage when it is remembered that this song is read by Israel at Passover time as a parable of God's love for Israel and of Israel's love for God. Israel then is called to love Yahweh with an erotic love of overwhelming power. She is to exult in her Lord with joy and gladness. Her worship is not to be servile obeisance but joyful attentiveness. Her rapture is to be like the rapture of sexuality. This commandment then specifically commends to Israel delight in Yahweh. It calls the hearer not to the solemn assembly but to the *ḥag*, the festival of merriment and joy.

Along with the joys of a wife, of course, go responsibilities. Just as a good wife will quite naturally, through the joy of love, harken to her husband's wishes, so Israel is also expected to keep her husband's commandments. The verb used here is *šamar*, a word already discussed briefly in chapter three.[8] In essence, it means not slavishly following orders, but listening carefully and responding. Israel is called, in effect, to keep Yahweh's commandments the way a good wife keeps her husband's house or garden. She is not just to go through the motions but to bestow upon her work the care which can only come from attentive love.

Yahweh's promised response to Israel's love is equally rich and full. The text says that he promises his *ḥesed*, his steadfast love, to thousands of those who love him and keep his commandments. The word *ḥesed* is one of those Hebrew words which it is virtually impossible to translate adequately. It can be rendered "ardor, zeal, steadfast love, loving kindness, tender mercy, benevolence,

---

8. Supra, pp. 60–61.

or benignity,"[9] but its connotations cannot be captured by any one of these words alone. Like the Greek *agape*, *ḥesed* implies an overflowing, benevolent love which seeks the good of the recipient. Normally, in human terms, it is the love which is shown by a good husband to his wife, by a father to his children, or by a king to his subjects. *Ḥesed* connotes concern for the other's well-being, succor, and kindness as well as delight. This is the kind of love with which Yahweh surrounds those who love him. Israel could never show *ḥesed* to God; it is not that kind of love. Invariably it is a love which is given by those who have to those who lack.

The Hebrew text clearly indicates that this *ḥesed* is more than simply an attitude on the part of Yahweh, for he promises to do *ḥesed*, to make his *ḥesed* concrete in action and event. Just as Israel's love entails keeping specific commandments and acting in certain ways, so Yahweh's love issues in specific works of loving kindness. The Revised Standard Version implies in its translation that what Yahweh promises is *ḥesed* to thousands of individuals, but the Hebrew does not seem to permit this interpretation. In the first place, God is speaking to Israel as a whole, not to individual persons. Furthermore, this phrase is obviously meant to contrast with the phrase which precedes it. Since these phrases are parallel, the passage should read:

> I the LORD your God am a jealous God, visiting the iniquities of the fathers upon the children to the third and the fourth generations of those who hate me but showing *ḥesed* to thousands of generations of those who love me and keep my commandments.

If this translation is correct, the promise is surely astounding. Yahweh is saying that one generation of fathers who show *'ahabah* to Yahweh will bring *ḥesed* upon their offspring for at least two thousand generations! God is saying, in effect, that the fruits of the love of him are nearly endless, from a human point of view. The man who truly loves God can be assured that he does not love in vain; Yahweh will see to that.

9. *Gesenius' Hebrew and Chaldee Lexicon*, pp. 293–94.

125

## 'EL ḴANA' AND COVENANTAL HATE

The name *'El Ḵana'*, Jealous God, which is employed in this commandment has long been a source of embarrassment to modern-day Christians, for it seems to portray Yahweh as a petulant, sulking husband who will not allow his wife any freedom lest she be unfaithful. Although this name does fit well into the metaphor of marriage as it is applied to the covenant, it is not meant to produce such repugnant connotations. On the contrary, God is seen to be *ḵana'* precisely because he has chosen Israel and offers to her his *ḥesed*. Therefore, a wiser translation of *ḵana'* might be "zealous" or "impassioned."[10]

Essentially *ḵana'* is meant to express the fact that God is a choosing, self-committing God who demands commitment. Like a human husband he expects from his wife the fidelity which issues from love. Hence, he confronts Israel with a radical either/or: either love me or hate me; there is no middle ground. Jealousy, then, is not a denial but rather an expression of God's choosing mercy. His wrath, which strikes down unfaithfulness, is but the other side of his love.

It is noteworthy that the Hebrew words for love and hate operate within the same frame of reference. *'Ahaḇah,* love, means, as it has already been pointed out, "desire, longing after, delight." It is the natural response of a wife for a husband. *Sanē',* to hate, when used to refer to the relation between a man and a woman regularly means "to feel a sexual revulsion for another." For instance, when Amnon, the son of David, had raped his half sister Tamar, it is said, "Then Amnon hated her *(yisna'eha)* with very great hatred *(sin'ah)*" (2 Samuel 13:15). The verb can also be used to refer to the hating of an enemy or of unrighteousness, but it may well be that the central paradigm is that of sexual revulsion.

Since the natural response of a wife for a husband is sexual desire and delight in him, any negation of that created urge is a

10. "Impassioned," which is used to translate *Ḵana'* in *The Torah,* recently published by the Jewish Publication Society, seems best.

form of hate. Outside of the marriage bond, a woman may quite naturally take a neutral attitude toward someone of the opposite sex, but once she has entered into marriage, such an uncommitted attitude is reprehensible. Neutrality in marriage is, in a very profound sense, a form of sexual revulsion.

A similar relation obtains between Israel and Yahweh. Israel marries Yahweh at Sinai and vows her love. If she does not continue to take delight in this relationship, if she is not positively attracted to her *"iš,"*[11] then she exhibits a lukewarm attitude which is equivalent to hate. Her festivals of mirth become merely "solemn assemblies"; her keeping of the law, but sullen obedience. And when joy is gone, idolatrous "whoring after other gods" is inevitable.

Hate is not an attitude which can be concealed. Invariably hate manifests itself as what is called sin or iniquity. The Hebrew language has, however, no one word which is quite equivalent to our word "sin," but contains a number of words, each with a slightly different set of connotations, which can be so translated. Among the most important of these words are *hata‘, peša‘,* and *‘awon* and their derivatives. Each can be used to describe within a particular metaphorical context Israel's relation to Yahweh.

The first and most common word which is translated "sin" is *hata‘.* In a "secular" context it means simply "to miss the mark, to miss the way, to stumble." Within a theological context *hata‘* is directly related to the metaphor of the *derek,* the way. All created beings, according to this metaphor, have a way marked out for them by their Creator; God has given to all men a *derek,* on which they should proceed. The righteous man walks on this way without stumbling and thus proceeds toward the destiny marked out for him by God. The man who wanders from the way, either consciously or inadvertently, becomes lost and thus is described as *hata‘,* sinful.

11. *Iš* means husband. Cf. Hosea 2:16.

Although Israel errs and strays and thus can be called *ḥata'*, a covenantal context is not necessarily implied. Since the pagans do not know Yahweh or his way they may exhibit *ḥata'* without even knowing it. There is no statement in the Old Testament that men outside of Israel *must* miss the way and stumble. Nevertheless, because they do not know God's way, they seem to do so inevitably. Israel's *ḥata'*, however, is often more rigorously denounced, because Israel has been shown the way of God and therefore ought to walk upon it.

The second word, *peša'*, means primarily "rebellion" or "transgression" and as such can be used in a thoroughly secular context to refer to a political dissident, an unruly son, a common criminal. When used theologically, it seems to "operate within" the metaphor of God as king. Since God is king of Israel and of the whole world, any act of disobedience is a *peša'*, rebellion against God. *Peša'*, unlike *ḥata'*, is almost always the result of willful and conscious choice. Although one can disobey the law without knowing it, rebellion usually involves a conscious act of defection and disloyalty. Only a positive act of clemency on the part of God can blot it out.

The third word, *'awon*, means perversity or depravity, for it is derived from the verb *'awah*, to bend or twist. One important feature of *'awon* is that it can refer to either the perversity itself or the punishment for the perversity. This distinction between sin and punishment, though necessary to make, is somewhat artificial, however, for the Israelite knew that perversity is its own punishment. The king punishes the rebel, but the perverted man, through his own twistedness, punishes himself.

*'Awon* is closely related metaphorically to the word *zedek*, righteousness, for *zedek* implies straightness or erectness. The man of *zedek* walks straight and tall; he exhibits wholeness of body and soul. The man of *'awon*, on the other hand, is twisted and bent. He is spiritually and even physically malformed. His desires are unruly; his vision, distorted; his relationships, corrupted. *'Awon* is also clearly related to the metaphor of marriage and sex-

ual relationship. The man or woman who no longer desires the opposite sex but is repulsed by the idea of sexual union is *'awon,* for the created impulses of man have been twisted.

It is, therefore, not surprising that *'awon* is used in the second commandment to refer to those who hate God. Since the natural tendency of Israel should be to love her husband, those who hate him are described as twisted. This twistedness is inevitably expressed in the concrete actions of the individual. Man is made in the image of God. Therefore, man's relation to God is reflected in his relations with other human beings. The man who hates God finds himself also perverted in his relations with other persons. Sexual perversions in particular are a reflection of sin.

The fact that *'awon* means both perversity and punishment also sheds light upon the statement that the *'awon* of the fathers shall be visited unto the third and fourth generations. In essence this is not so much a threat as a description of what, in fact, is the case.[12] Because perversity is infectious, twisted fathers inevitably produce perversity in their children. It takes about three or four generations for the effect of a particular perversity to wear itself out.

The Decalogue does not speak only of the psychological relationship between father and son. This commandment refers also, and perhaps primarily, to the relation between whole generations. The evil which our fathers did bears bitter fruit in our generation. We wrestle with the problems created by their *'awon* in every social sphere. The tragedy is that we, in turn, pass on the fruits of our perversity to the generations which succeed us and so create new, seemingly unsolvable problems for our descendants.

This conception of the infectious nature of sin provides a clue for the understanding of the biblical interpretations of human history. The Book of Judges, for instance, identifies the chief *'awon* of that day as idolatry. Worship of the *Ba'alim* produced a people who were politically disunited, sexually perverted, and militarily weak; defeat at the hands of the Midianites, Ammonites,

12. Dorothy L. Sayers, *The Mind of the Maker* (New York: Harcourt, Brace and Co., 1941), p. 12.

and Philistines was the natural fruit of this *'awon*. The Books of Kings identify the central sin as political and religious disunity which was symbolized by the refusal of the northern kings to worship at one central shrine. This perversity is seen to be the kernel of sin which brought disaster to Israel at the hands of Damascus and Assyria. Neither the Deuteronomic writers of Israel's history nor prophets such as Amos thought of God's judgment as "breaking into" history. The punishment which befalls one generation is regarded as the natural fruit of the sins of the previous generations.[13]

Those who criticize God for punishing innocent children for the sins of their fathers, then, may express true moral concern, but miss the descriptive nature of the commandment. The fact that sin is infectious and that children suffer for the sins of their fathers may be lamentable, but it cannot be denied, for it is just as much a "law" of psychology and history as it is the "revealed" will of God. Every generation bears, in one way or another, the sins of the preceding generations upon its back.

This fact of life provides the biblical rationale for righteousness and obedience. The Old Testament, at least, offers no succulent, heavenly rewards to the pious; no threat of eternal hell for the unrighteous. It simply reminds the believer that his actions will have consequences which will extend far beyond his own lifetime. Not only is *'awon* its own punishment, but the guilty man is also assured that his children and his grand-children and his great-grandchildren will suffer in one way or another for his perversity.

---

13. One common image for describing Israel's punishment is that of a prostitute in the throes of childbirth. Israel has played the harlot and her consequent pain is the fruit of her disobedience. Although Israel never developed a "doctrine" of original sin, she often came close to it. The sins of the fathers pervert the sons. They, in turn, pass on the *'awon* in new forms to their children. Although the effects of one particular type of *'awon* wear out in three or four generations, man can never quite free himself from the cycle of guilt and punishment, for one *'awon* begets another. Not until the writings of Paul, however, are the rigorous implications of this view of man made clear. (Cf. Romans 2.)

## Chapter 7

# WHAT'S IN A NAME?

You shall not take the name of the LORD your God in vain: for the LORD will not hold him guiltless who takes his name in vain (Exodus 20:7).

Even the most superficial reader of Scripture soon becomes aware of the emphasis placed upon names throughout the Old Testament. On nearly every page, one is confronted by a host of personal names denoting human beings, places, and even things. Frequently the name is accompanied by an explanation of its etymological derivation so that its meaning is clear to the reader. Although such derivations often seem farfetched when the Hebrew is studied carefully, the fact remains that for Israel the meaning of names was supremely important. A name was never regarded as just an arbitrary token used to denote an individual object; it was a means through which the mysterious existence of *someone* was revealed.

Perhaps the best way to understand the biblical attitude toward names is to contrast it with the approach taken by both the Greek philosophers and modern scientists. For the Greek philosopher the most important intellectual enterprise was abstraction and generalization. In his search for knowledge the philosopher sought for general concepts to express those features which various substances might have in common. For Plato not only knowledge but reality is to be found in these universal forms; the material world of uniqueness and individuality is illusion.[1] Aristotle did not deny so decisively the reality of this world, for he regarded form (the idea) and matter (the principle of individuation) as inseparable. Nonetheless, he believed that all true knowledge is reducible to a series of statements concerning class inclusion and exclusion.[2] The statement, "Socrates is mortal," could, for purposes of "knowing," be reduced to the form "Some A is B." Thus for Aristotle, and for Western philosophy in general, the name was sacrificed upon the altar of the concept.[3]

Modern scientists and philosophers have revised Aristotelian logic somewhat and have developed new terminology by which to describe and explain the nature of things. Aristotle's philosophical vocabulary is often criticized as misleading or inappropriate, for it seems to lead to a basic misunderstanding of the universe. The essential impulse of Greek philosophy, however, remains as a partial basis for modern science. As Hans Reichenbach, the articulate spokesman for scientific philosophy says, "the essence of knowledge is generalization."[4] Greek philosophical vocabulary is attacked by Reichenbach as pseudoscientific but is replaced by the more quantitatively exact formulations of modern mathematics. For him also the name must be sacrificed for the sake of the generalization.

The Israelite generalized about his experience too. He used abstract nouns and verbs, for man can only really communicate about the world in this way. Still, he knew that abstract words can never capture the unique existence of anything. He spoke of

1. Plato, *The Republic,* Bk. 7.

2. Aristotle, *Posterior Analytics,* passim.

3. For centuries there has been an existentialist "undercurrent" in Western philosophy which has given a place to the reality of personal uniqueness, but, on the whole, until the twentieth century such an emphasis has been overshadowed by the abstracting, essentialist tendencies of Greek philosophy.

4. Hans Reichenbach, *The Rise of Scientific Philosophy* (Berkeley, Calif.: University of California Press, 1963), p. 5.

mountains, but he also knew that there is, ultimately, no such reality as "mountainness." Or perhaps better, it never occurred to him that such a general concept could have reality. For him there was only this particular mountain and that particular mountain. Because each existent thing is unique, the only accurate "definition," if one wants to call it that, is an ostensive one. Thus, when he wished to speak of anything he said "there" *(šam)* and gave a name *(šem)*.

This is not to say, however, that the Israelite was a nominalist rather than a realist.[5] Although a nominalist sees the difficulties involved in making generalizations about the universe and therefore eschews any attempt to find true universals, he still moves in the realm of objective, generalizing philosophy. Knowledge is conceived as a series of descriptive, albeit particular, statements about the world, rather than as a personal confrontation with the world. In the last analysis William of Ockham, the nominalist, was still much closer to Aristotle than to Moses and the prophets.

Naming is, in the Bible, seen to be one of man's primary functions in life.

> So out of the ground the LORD God formed every beast of the field and every bird of the air, and brought them to the man to see what he would call them; and whatever the man called every living creature, that was its name (Genesis 2:19).

Through naming, man, like God, creates order out of the chaos of experience, but this order is not the abstract order of the philosopher or scientist. Instead, it is a personal order, for whenever a person truly names he says implicitly "Thou," not "It." The world is filled with unique existences, each with his own specific name. A name is a sign that that which is named is more than an object which exists indifferently in the world. That which is named confronts man with a dimension of existence which transcends mere

5. I use these terms rather loosely to signify two schools of thought. The realists, who dominated early Medieval philosophizing, emphasized the reality of universals. The nominalists described universals as mere "breathings of the voice."

objecthood. The name is an attempt to capture and express the quality and the intensity of this unique confrontation.

It is not surprising, then, that great attention is paid to the names of men in the Bible. Whenever a child is born a name which expresses something of his immediate impact upon the family is usually chosen.[6] It is meant to convey the existence of the person's *nepeš*; it is the vocalization of his very self. As Pedersen says, for an Israelite, "to know the name of a man is the same as to know his essence."[7] I would only qualify this by saying that it is the existence rather than the essence of the person which is denoted. One can know someone "essentially" (that is, his attributes) without knowing him existentially at all.

Because a man's name is closely associated with his very self, it must be changed if that reality is decisively altered. In particular, since a man's self finds its full meaning only in relation to God, the source of existence, any vital change in that relationship necessitates a new name. Hence Abram, after having entered into covenant with God, is renamed Abraham. Jacob wrestles victoriously by the river Jabbok and is renamed Israel. Place names are also sometimes changed because of an important revelatory event. Jacob dreams of God at Luz and so renames the place Bethel, the house of God. Moses sees the burning bush *(seneh)* on the slopes of Horeb. Thus the mountain is renamed Sinai after the locus of the event.

## THE NAME OF GOD

Given this attitude toward the importance of names it is not strange that for the people of Israel the name of God was also of great significance. The Greek, philosophical way of speaking of the Deity was and is invariably abstract and negative. Christian theologians have, in general, followed this approach, describing God as "infinite in being and perfection, a most pure spirit, invisible,

6. Cf. Genesis 30 in which Jacob's wives name some of his children.
7. Johannes Pedersen, *Israel: Its Life and Culture,* 4 vols. (London: Oxford University Press, 1926), 1:245.

... immutable, immense, eternal, incomprehensible. . . ."[8] Although such a description, when properly understood, may be useful, the Bible avoids such language almost completely. God is praised for his love, his righteousness, and his mercy; his wrath is mentioned with fear. His actions among men are exalted and glorified, but his essence is left undefined. The most that Israel will say is that Yahweh is *'Elohim,* the Power of all powers.

When Israel wishes to speak of God, she points to the concrete events of her life which have revealed him to her. She says *šam,* there he is, and names his name. Israel, of course, does not simply make up names for God. She uses names which doubtless had a long, prerevelatory history. Even Yahweh, God's most sacred covenantal name, was used in one form or another by pagans for centuries. Still, when Israel employs the name after the exodus, it has a distinct, revealed meaning unknown to its pagan users. Now this name is revealed to be the covenantal name through which Israel, the bride, can address her bridegroom. This is the name which he bestows upon her and in so doing makes her his own. Only those who have truly heard God speak and have entered into covenant with him know his name. For others it is but meaningless babbling upon the lips.

As the second commandment implies, God himself is incomprehensible and unimaginable. Israel is, therefore, commanded not to make any graven image or likeness of him. She is, however, given the name, the holy tetragrammaton, which expresses in mysterious brevity the meaning given to Israel by God through the exodus-Sinai event. The name "Yahweh" is the memory and revelation of God in capsule form. The name, indeed, is conceived as the presence, the *šekinah* of God himself, for where the name is truly spoken there is the remembrance of the word which God spoke to Israel. And when God's word to Israel in the past is remembered, God speaks in the present. Thus the name of God is Israel's most sacred possession. It is the word of faith *par excellence;* the rest

8. Gerald I. Williamson, *Westminster Confession of Faith* (Nutley, N.J.: Presbyterian and Reformed Pub. Co., 1965), ch. II, 1.

of the Old Testament is but an elaboration and explanation of what that name means.

## TAKING UP THE NAME

The prohibition of taking up the name of Yahweh in vain is often interpreted to mean simply, "Do not use the name of God profanely, as pepper on your speech." And surely, the commandment does imply this, for it prohibits all vulgar and degrading uses of the name of God. Such usage, in fact, is a sure indication that the speaker is not a true member of Israel, for his faith is gone. He no longer hears the word which binds Israel to her God and therefore no longer senses the significance of the name he speaks.

This commandment, however, is far more than a prohibition of what today is called "cursing." The term *lašav'*, which is here translated "in vain," has connotations not obviously implied in the English, for the word *šav'*, can be translated as "wickedness or iniquity, falsehood, a lie; emptiness, vanity, nothingness."[9] Thus the meaning of the commandment is manifold; in its terseness it speaks to a variety of situations. Ludwig Koehler has commented that it is noteworthy that there is no commandment in the Decalogue forbidding lying.[10] In one sense this is true, for there is no commandment saying directly, "Thou shalt not lie." Nor is there much concern in the Bible for the little fibs and exaggerations which we all inevitably make. It is not true, however, that lying, in the full-blown, pernicious sense remains unprohibited. Not only is the bearing of false witness against one's neighbor denounced. In this commandment, any statement which deceives is forbidden. The Israelite who speaks the name of the Lord must act in truth, for the Lord's name is truth. To swear falsely and yet bear God's name is to break the covenant of God.

9. *Gesenius' Hebrew and Chaldee Lexicon to the Old Testament Scriptures,* ed. Samuel Prideaux Tregelles (Grand Rapids, Mich.: Wm. B. Eerdmans, 1954), p. 807.
10. Ludwig Koehler, *Old Testament Theology,* trans. A. S. Todd (Philadelphia: Westminster Press, 1958), p. 251 n.

This commandment not only prohibits profanity and lying. Perhaps most important, it forbids all religious hypocrisy and tepidness. The verb *nasa'*, which is here translated "take," connotes more than simply to use. It is a verb which is used to mean "lift up your hand," "lift up your voice," or "lift up your prayers." Often it is employed in cultic situations. To lift up the name of God, then, might well mean to worship God in the cult. In effect the commandment says, if you use the name of God, be sure that you mean what you say. It is directed against the priest of Yahweh who lifts up God's name in order to further his own ambitions, against the elder who parades his religion in order to win friends and influence people, against the theologian who has become so accustomed to the name of God that it rolls off his tongue without thought or reverence.

In other words, far from being a rather limited prohibition of profanity, this commandment has far-reaching significance for all of life. Israel, as the bride of Yahweh, is called to treasure his name, to use it with honor and respect, and to bear it honestly and prudently. Yahweh has spoken to Israel and has made her his own; this joyful reality she must acknowledge by glorifying his name and the *dabar* of hope which it represents.

"For the Lord will not hold him guiltless who takes his name in vain." Unlike many ancient codes of law there are no curses and few threats contained in the Decalogue. Only in the second and third commandments are there statements describing God's reaction to an infringement of the commandments. For this reason, the phrase we are now considering stands out emphatically, almost terrifyingly. The phrase "will not hold him guiltless" bears no indication of what the exact punishment will be and, for that reason, perhaps, seems particularly ominous.

The verb *yenakeh,* translated here "will (not) hold him guiltless," comes from the verb *nakah* which means "to be pure, innocent, free from punishment, pardoned." Although the Revised Standard Version offers an accurate translation, it misses something of the cultic significance of the word. The sentence might well be paraphrased, "Yahweh will not purify him who lifts up the name of God without sincerity." In other words, this can be interpreted to mean that God will not look with favor upon hypocritical religious acts.

Amos, then, is just reiterating the meaning of this commandment when he proclaims God's word:

> I hate, I despise your feasts,
>> and I take no delight in your solemn assemblies.
>
> Even though you offer me your burnt offerings and
>> cereal offerings,
>> I will not accept them,
>
> and the peace offerings of your fatted beasts
>> I will not look upon.
>
> Take away from me the noise of your songs;
>> to the melody of your harps I will not listen.
>
> But let justice roll down like waters,
>> and righteousness like an ever-flowing stream
>>
>> (Amos 5:21–24).

Israel has failed to hear God's covenantal word; although she continues to worship Yahweh, she fails to obey him. Therefore, says Amos, you are hypocrites and the Lord will not hold you guiltless.

I have already spoken in favor of cultic religion in chapter five and I surely do not wish to retract it now. The Old Testament throughout accepts religion as a necessary and important part of human life. Nevertheless, it is significant that this commandment, which contains one of the few possible references to cultic practices in the Decalogue, is a word of warning. Israel knew the value and the inevitability of religion. She knew that her faith in Yahweh needed formal religious expression. There must be festivals, sacrifices, assemblies, and chants. But Israel at her best also knew how easily all these accoutrements of the faith can be corrupted and emptied of their true meaning. When this commandment is not obeyed, they become merely a snare and a delusion through which people are assured that they are faithful believers when, as a matter of fact, they know nothing at all of Yahweh. The third commandment is a solemn warning of this danger.

But why the terrifying threat? Why include here the stern admonition when no such admonition follows, for instance, the sixth commandment? Precisely because this commandment is so easily broken. Murder, adultery, theft, and the like are overtly willed acts. Even belief in other gods is usually a conscious deed. Hypocrisy in religion, however, can begin almost without notice. One can use God's name irreverently without even realizing that the deed has been done. Therefore, it is particularly necessary to remind the believer of the consequences.

Perhaps the word consequences is more apt than the word threat. This is not so much a threat to alarm as it is simply a description of what the actual results of taking God's name in vain really are. It is a reminder that when God's name is used lightly the faith engendered by God's voice is soon eroded away, the redemptive power of God's act of manumission is lost, and the believer soon finds himself back in the house of bondage to other gods.

# PART III:

# ADAM

"Remember the sabbath day, to keep it holy. Six days you shall labor, and do all your work; but the seventh day is a sabbath to the LORD your God; in it you shall not do any work, you, or your son, or your daughter, your manservant, or your maidservant, or your cattle, or the sojourner who is within your gates; for in six days the LORD made heaven and earth, the sea, and all that is in them, and rested the seventh day; therefore the LORD blessed the sabbath day and hallowed it.

Honor your father and your mother, that your days may be long in the land which the LORD your God gives you.

You shall not kill.
You shall not commit adultery.
You shall not steal.
You shall not bear false witness against your neighbor.

You shall not covet your neighbor's house; you shall not covet your neighbor's wife, or his manservant, or his maidservant, or his ox, or his ass, or anything that is your neighbor's."

## Chapter 8

# THE SABBATH WAS
# MADE FOR MAN

"Remember the Sabbath day, to keep it holy. Six days you shall labor, and do all your work; but the seventh day is a sabbath to the LORD your God; in it you shall not do any work, you, or your son, or your daughter, your manservant, or your maidservant, or your cattle, or the sojourner who is within your gates; for in six days the LORD made heaven and earth, the sea, and all that is in them, and rested the seventh day; therefore the LORD blessed the sabbath day and hallowed it"
(Exodus 20:8–11).

## "REMEMBER"

Although scholars debated heatedly in the past about the origins of the Sabbath celebration, it is reasonably clear today that it did not originate among the Israelites. Israel, to be sure, infused the observance of the day with its own meaning, but the practice of setting aside one day in seven as special was not invented by her. This is, as a matter of fact, true of most of Israel's religious festivals and traditions. A custom such as resting on appointed days could no more be invented at a particular time than could the custom of concluding the harvest season with a festival. Even those celebrations based exclusively upon the remembrances of some historical event tended to absorb practices which antedated them. All of Israel's major festivals, though commemorating events, are also based upon ancient holy days which in origin were pagan through and through.

We now know that this was as true for the Sabbath as it was for Tabernacles and Passover. When Abraham arrived in Canaan he doubtless found the Canaanites already observing a seven day week and a yearly calendar based upon the pentecontad, a fifty day period composed of seven weeks of seven days plus one day of festival.[1] Morgenstern writes:

Actually the sabbath had its origin in a unique and rather primitive calendar, distinctly agricultural in character, which was current among the various West Semitic peoples until approximately 1000 B.C.—i.e. until some three centuries, more or less, after the settlement of the Hebrews in Palestine and the adjustment of the majority of their tribes, particularly those dwelling in the more fertile central and N. sections of the country, where farming was naturally the dominant occupation, to Canaanite civilization. This calendar was based upon and recorded the successive stages in the planting, ripening, harvesting, and use of the annual crop. It was one of the institutions of Canaanite culture which these Hebrew newcomers borrowed.[2]

Some scholars in the past have argued that Israel learned of the Sabbath from the Babylonians who observed the *shabbatu,* a day of evil portent when work was avoided because of the unluckiness of the day. Probably, however, the truth is that Israel and the Babylonians derived their respective observances from the older West Semitic culture which antedated both.[3]

The Babylonians seem to have preserved the meaning of the earlier observances more closely than did Israel. For most ancient Semitic peoples the number seven was not only mysterious but

1. J. Morgenstern, "Sabbath," in *The Interpreter's Dictionary of the Bible,* 4 vols., ed. G. A. Buttrick et al. (New York: Abingdon Press, 1962), 4:135–136.
2. Ibid., p. 135. Used by permission.
3. Ibid.

ominous and unlucky. Hence the seventh day was regarded as a time when evil spirits were abroad and when it was, therefore, unpropitious to work. Israel retained a sense of the mystery which the number seven elicited among ancient people but seems to have discarded almost completely any notion than the number is unlucky.[4] Surely, there is no hint in Scripture that the Sabbath was a day of evil portent. On the contrary, the Sabbath is invariably described as a day of rejoicing and gladness.

The fact that Israel adopted a long-standing preexodus practice is signified by the first word of the fourth commandment, "remember." God does not institute this observance as something new but instead calls Israel to return to a practice with which she is already well acquainted but which she is called to infuse with a new and distinctive meaning. Gone is any mention of the demonic forces which were said to control the seventh day. Israel is now to rejoice in the fact that Yahweh has conquered the pseudodivinities of paganism.

It is often argued that since the celebration of the Sabbath is closely related to the agricultural, rather than the nomadic life, it is very doubtful that Israel could have celebrated the Sabbath in the wilderness. Although this argument is quite cogent and accepted by many, the possibility that Israel already had been introduced to the Sabbath before her descent into Egypt is important to remember. Is it not possible that Israel, in her attempt to recover this lost tradition, tried to celebrate the seventh day in the wilderness even though the new context drastically limited the nature of the celebration?

Exodus 16 tells the strange and, to some, unbelievable story of the gift of manna. We are told that not only did the Israelites receive manna from God but that the manna observed the Sab-

4. Morgenstern argues (Ibid., pp. 136–137) that the fact that only six of the seven nations inhabiting the land of Canaan at the time of the conquest are usually mentioned indicates that Israel may have regarded it as unlucky to list all seven. Actually, however, all seven names are listed together in Deuteronomy 7:1 and in Joshua 3:10 and 24:11. The omission of the Girgashites from most lists may simply be due to the fact that this group of people was rather small and insignificant.

bath too. On the sixth day Israel was able to collect twice as much manna. Although normally the manna could not be preserved, it was on this occasion. Furthermore, no manna "fell" on the Sabbath and those who searched for it found none. As it has already been pointed out, not all of the aspects of this story need to be regarded as fictitious. G. Ernest Wright says:

> Thus manna is still produced today in the tamarisk thickets of the valleys of central Sinai. One man may collect over a kilogram a day at the peak of the season in June. It is a honey-like substance, ranging in size from pinhead to pea. It is produced by two species of scale-like insect which must suck in large quantities of sap in order to secure the nitrogen they need and then give off what they do not need in the form of honeydew excretion. Rapid evaporation changes the drops quickly into sticky solids which may be gathered.[5]

What is apparently unbelievable then is not that there was manna but that the manna obeyed the Sabbath law. Whether any naturalistic explanation will be found for the fact that on one particular day manna was not available for gathering but that the extra manna which they gathered the preceding day did not become wormy I do not know. Such an explanation would be somewhat beside the point anyway. What is important is that Israel herself remembered that the Sabbath had been celebrated before the covenant at Sinai had been made. If the story can be interpreted literally, Moses seems to have taken this fortuitous opportunity as a signal to reinstitute a custom which had apparently been long neglected. The abundance of manna on that sixth day and the absence of it on the seventh was taken to be a reminder from God that the Sabbath should again be observed. It is noteworthy that there is no indication that this strange phenomenon was repeated each week.

5. From *Biblical Archaeology*, by G. Ernest Wright, pp. 64–65. Published simultaneously in the United States by The Westminster Press, Philadelphia, and Gerald Duckworth & Co., Ltd., London, England, 1957. Used by permission.

## THE MEANING OF THE SABBATH

Many scholars argue that the original commandment was limited to the words: "Remember the Sabbath to keep it holy," and that the following clauses were added later. The fact that the Sabbath was already observed by the Canaanites calls this thesis into question. If Israel wished to reinterpret the pagan custom, as she usually did, it was important for her to make clear what the meaning of the Sabbath was to be for her. The opening line, however, is very noncommittal. To be sure it means that some days should be set apart as special, but that is about all that is said. One may well suspect, therefore, that unless Israel simply took over the pagan custom as it was—which is doubtful—the original commandment must have contained some explanatory statement.

Verses nine and ten explain briefly how the Sabbath is to be kept holy. Verse eleven then gives the justification. Although this order is quite proper, it is best for our purposes to reverse it, for only in the light of the "why" of the commandment can we come to a full appreciation of the "how." The explanation in verse eleven is so familiar to most readers that it is a great temptation to pass over it without much thought, but when we contemplate what is said the justification seems very queer indeed.

> For in six days the LORD made heaven and earth, the sea, and all that is in them, and rested the seventh day; therefore, the LORD blessed the sabbath day and hallowed it (Exodus 20:11).

What can this possibly mean? If God is the total cause of the universe upon whom all things depend at every moment for existence, what can it mean to say that God "rested on the seventh day"? If God stopped creating would not the world simply disappear? This is a difficult problem which drives us to the very heart of the commandment.

The word which is translated "rest" both in this verse and in Genesis 2:2 is *šabat* which means "to cease, to desist, to leave off, to rest." It may or may not be etymologically related to *šaba'*, seven, but surely the alliterative association is intended. In any event, the seventh day is the day when God ceased doing what he was doing. What does this mean? The first chapter of Genesis traces the development of greater and greater order and of higher and higher forms of life in the universe. God speaks and order is created out of chaos. On the sixth day, God creates the cattle, the creeping things, and the beasts of the earth. Then, as the apex of his work he creates man in his own image and likeness. Until this point God had pronounced his work good; now he proclaims it very good. Then he ceases and desists. Because of his infinite power, God could go right on creating higher and higher forms of life. Adam would then be but a pawn in the hands of these superior powers. But God does not. After he creates man, he ceases and desists.

There is good reason, therefore, for Jesus' assertion that "the sabbath was made for man, not man for the sabbath" (Mark 2:27). If the interpretation given above is correct, the Sabbath is meant to be a day when man's dignity as the highest of God's creatures is celebrated. Man is reminded by this day, which is meant as a sign, an *'ot* from God,[6] that he is not just a slave; he is the image and likeness of God. Although he is meant to work—for God himself works—he is also meant to be free. Thus, far from being intended as a day of dullness and oppression, the Sabbath is meant to be a day of great joy and gladness. It is meant to be the celebration of the fact that man alone is made in the image of God, that man alone is commanded to have dominion over creation, that man alone has a special dignity and God-given glory which he ought neither forget nor neglect.

### "SIX DAYS YOU SHALL LABOR, AND DO ALL YOUR WORK"

Although no major tradition has considered verse nine as a separate commandment, the fourth "word" is really not one but two. Not only is Israel commanded to remember the Sabbath day; she is also commanded to labor. Why? Why does God specifically command Israel to labor six days a week? The explanation for this commandment is also found in the myth of creation already

6. Exodus 31:13, 17.

mentioned in connection with the Sabbath. This myth, after tracing out the formation of the world and all the host of living creatures in it, continues:

> And on the seventh day God finished his work which he had done, and he rested on the seventh day from all his work which he had done. So God blessed the seventh day and hallowed it, because on it God rested from all his work which he had done in creation (Genesis 2:2).

It is striking that the fact that God works is underlined so repeatedly in this verse. God is not seen as the passive, inert deity of Plotinus nor as the blissful state of unconscious nirvana sought for by the Buddhists. No, Yahweh is a God who works, acts, does and because man is made in the image of God, he can work and create as well.

How strange it is that most people think that the Garden of Eden was a place of restful inactivity when, as a matter of fact, the Bible distinctly denies this! Adam was created, not just to "vegetate" or even to offer prayers all day, but to till the garden and keep it. He named the animals and thus ordered his world; he engaged in the tasks of the agriculturalist. It was only after man's act of disobedience, when he gained the so-called knowledge of good and evil, that man began to consider his work a curse (Genesis 3:17–19). In the beginning, it was not so. Man was made to work and thereby to reflect God, the creator.

With the Sinaitic covenant, God and man are reconciled and therefore the curse of man's work is taken away. No longer need men regard toil as a burden and a punishment. Men are called to labor and do their work, not just as a means of eking out a miserable (or prosperous) existence, but for the glory of God. Israel is called to find her dignity in her secular existence.

Two types of work are distinguished in this commandment. The first, which is indicated by the word *ta'abod,* means simply to labor. Although it can be used in a variety of ways *ta'abod* usually connotes hard physical work, even servitude. The second type of work, expressed by the Hebrew *m<sup>e</sup>la'kteka,* also has a wide range of connotations, but implies primarily a more creative activity, such as that exhibited by an artisan. It may be that two words are used simply for emphasis and that no distinction between them is implied. More likely, however, both are used in order to indicate that in both hard physical labor and in creative activity God's own work is reflected. Even the slave and hired hand reflect God in their toiling. It is true that God, in Genesis 2:2, does $m^e la'$ $kah$ but does not $'abad$. God's work is entirely creative; it would seem incomprehensible to think of him as slaving. Exodus 20 makes clear, however, that this does not mean that physical labor is somehow beneath man's dignity. It also is a reflection of God's image.

This attitude toward labor, though not absolutely unique, is surely quite unusual among the peoples of the earth. For most of the $goi'im$ the ideal state is a life of leisure, the condition enjoyed by the wealthy and powerful. Aristotle, in fact, says that man cannot be happy without some leisure.[8] Hence, he excludes from the ranks of the happy all slaves and poor men. Nearly every non-Judeo-Christian religious tradition has concurred with Aristotle. Not only does man need much leisure time for contemplation and religious duties if he is to be truly holy: Paradise is normally pictured as a place of rest and relaxation, not labor.

For the Bible, such is not the case. The end of man is not seen as blissful ease but as a city, the new Jerusalem, in which creative work goes on. In this world, man needs the Sabbath to restore his well-being, but he also needs to work if he is to truly live as the image of God. When man is denied this vehicle for his energy and creativity a spiritual crisis can be the only result.

### OTHERS

As we have just noted, according to Scripture, man is made to work and loses his dignity if he does not do so. Still, this commandment also affirms that man is more than a worker. In fact, it is a

---

7. In the New Testament Jesus is implicitly identified as the suffering servant spoken of by Deutero-Isaiah, but as such Jesus acts as the quintessence of Israel. He is the servant (slave) of God, but God is not the slave.

8. Aristotle, *Nichomachean Ethics,* Bk. I, ch. 10; Bk. X, ch. 7.

reminder that although work is man's blessing, if man binds himself too closely to his work, his dignity will be turned to slavery. The Sabbath is meant to be a periodic sign that man is free from the bondage of work. All men, no matter what their station, should be allowed a day when they can recollect their value as men rather than as cogs in the industries of the objective world.

In verse ten this theme is elaborated very specifically. In a document as terse as this Decalogue, an enumeration such as is found here, stands out with stark clarity. This, undoubtedly, is the intent. The Bible accepts, in general, the fact that there will inevitably be a kind of stratification of society. There will always be some who rule and some who serve; some who are parents and some who are children; some who are members of society and some who are foreigners. The Sabbath Day, however, is a revelation that such distinctions are only for human convenience and well-being. Before God all men have dignity. Therefore, the freedom from work which the Sabbath provides is not restricted to the ruler, the master, and the parent. These persons are commanded specifically to guarantee that the Sabbath rest will be provided for the child, the servant, and the foreigner as well. On this day the distinctions between the mighty and the weak are negated; the slave, like his master, can enjoy leisure.

This general interpretation seems to be substantiated quite well by the alternative explanation of the commandment given in the Deuteronomic Decalogue. It is interesting that one of the very few differences between the Decalogues of Exodus 20 and Deuteronomy 5 is to be found in the justification given to this commandment. It is the only variation which can be said to be major. The text of Deuteronomy 5:15 reads as follows:

> You shall remember that you were a servant in the land of Egypt, and the LORD your God brought you out thence with a mighty hand and an outstretched arm; therefore the LORD your God commanded you to keep the sabbath day.

Here the fourth commandment is far more closely related to the exodus event in which God spoke. Israel is called to celebrate the

Sabbath as a reminder of her freedom from slavery which God wrought through the exodus. Each Sabbath day should be marked by a return of that feeling of glorious relief experienced as Israel crossed the Sea of Reeds. Israel is called to rejoice that her days of servitude are over and to consider with compassion the servitude of others.

Which of these explanations came first is difficult to say. Since the first chapter of Genesis is usually said to have been written during the exilic period, it may be that the justifying phrase in Exodus is quite late. Although such an argument bears consideration, it is not necessarily correct, for the liturgy of creation found in the opening chapter of Genesis may well be based upon older traditions. It could indeed be an expansion upon this phrase of this commandment or upon an even older source.

Such a question, however, is really irrelevant for our consideration here. What is of interest is that the two explanations found in Exodus and Deuteronomy nicely complement each other. The Deuteronomic explanation is, perhaps, clearer because it relates the commandment much more closely to the word-event of the exodus. In its light it is far easier to see the basic point that the Sabbath is meant to be a celebration of man's freedom and dignity. Its chief defect (if I can speak in those terms) is that it seems to give dignity primarily to Israel alone. Although Deuteronomy mentions the sojourner (the *ger*) within the gates as also being graced by the Sabbath law, the emphasis falls upon Israel's freedom. The explanation in Exodus, on the other hand, is more cryptic and less easily interpreted, but it is also far more cosmic in scope, for it includes all men everywhere. Deuteronomy reveals how the Sabbath word is derived from the word of "bringing out." Exodus reveals that the word of the "bringing out" is the same word as that spoken to all men through creation. It is a reminder that the word spoken to Israel in a particular event bears meaning for all men.

The fourth commandment is, in any event, far from being an invitation to the slavery of dullness. Rather, it is the cornerstone of biblical humanism. In recent years many important theologians have placed strong emphasis upon the "negative aspects" of the biblical doctrine of man. We have heard, almost *ad nauseum* about man's propensity to sin, about his existential predicament, about his insurmountable pride. And surely this word of "No" has been well taken. Against the vapid liberalism of the first decades of this century neoorthodoxy came as a needed breath of realism.

As true as neoorthodoxy's analysis of man's nature is, the truth of the doctrine of original sin must not blind us to the other, equally important side of the biblical message. Man may be perverse and corrupt, but he is still the apex of God's creation. He is made in the image of God and is the recipient of his *hesed*. God has made for man a day as a sign of this dignity. He has blessed the Sabbath and has set it apart as holy that man may remember his own grandeur and give thanks to his creator.

### CATTLE

Included among those not to work on the Sabbath are not only the various persons of the household but also the cattle. The reasons for this are not difficult to understand. Because man is made in the image of God, he has the ability to dominate creation, to domesticate cattle, and to till the soil. This means, in effect, that both cattle and the land are involved in and affected by man's creativity. Therefore, all domesticated animals, because they have been made "unnatural" by man's dominion over them must be given an opportunity to rest. The wild deer need not celebrate the Sabbath because it does not truly work. The ox, on the other hand, is forced to pull heavy loads and thus, in a qualified sense, works. Although cattle do not reflect God's image directly, they do, nonetheless, participate in labor and thus must share in the benefits of the Sabbath.

The land, of course, cannot rest every seventh day, for the tempo of vegetative life is much slower. Even so, the land is affected by man's ability to work and must be given a Sabbath too. Although no mention is made of the Sabbatical year in this Decalogue, it would seem that at quite an early time, the Israelites developed the practice of letting the land lie fallow every seventh year.

The practice of celebrating the Sabbatical year suffered many vicissitudes and was probably not recognized in all eras. As Israel became more urban its celebration became less relevant and more difficult to carry out. The custom was, however, revived at several different times during the history of Israel and was practiced in postexilic Judaism. In 1 Maccabees 6:49, 53–54 we are told that Beth-zur fell to Antiochus IV because the food supply of the garrison was soon exhausted since it was the Sabbatical year. After the fall of Jerusalem in A.D. 70, however, Jews became more widely dispersed and it became impossible to observe this year in any strict sense. This does not mean that the idea of a Sabbatical year was completely forgotten. Even today many farmers, though unacquainted with the original law, still find it important to let their land renew itself periodically by allowing a field to lie fallow. The religious meaning of the commandment is largely lost, but the "natural law" is still recognized.

### "THEREFORE THE LORD BLESSED THE SABBATH DAY AND HALLOWED IT"

It is unfortunate, but not surprising, that the words "bless" *(barak)* and blessing *(berakah)* have largely lost their original meaning for us. Religious people still say a "blessing" before meals. The benediction which concludes a service is given in the form of a blessing. But the rich meaning of the Hebrew word is gone. For the Israelite a blessing was far more than a kind word said or a prayer offered. For him blessing meant power. Johannes Pedersen writes:

> The soul is a whole saturated with power. It is the same power which acts in the centre and far out in the periphery; as far as the soul extends. It makes the soul grow and prosper, in order

that it may maintain itself and do its work in the world. This vital power, without which no living being can exist, is called by Israelites, *berakah,* blessing.[9]

Blessings are not restricted to man. The blessing of the antelope is its swiftness; of the fox, its cunning. The grape is blessed with juiciness; the honey, with sweetness. Mankind's blessing, however, surpasses all the rest.

"And God blessed them, and God said to them, 'Be fruitful and multiply, and fill the earth and subdue it . . .'" (Genesis 1:28). The power of fertility and of transcendent dominion over the earth is man's blessing, his *berakah.* This is what distinguishes him from the beasts of the field and the other creatures of the earth. If man is to be man this blessing must be fulfilled. The suppression of man's blessing means, in effect, the denial of God's will. Hence neither celibacy nor the cloistered life of prayer were held in high esteem by Israel. Man serves God best, he reflects his blessing most, in the raising of a family and in work.

Not only is mankind blessed in general; individuals receive individual blessings which distinguish them from the rest of humanity. Perhaps the most famous and important blessing of the Bible is to be found in Genesis 12:1–3:

> Now the LORD said to Abram, "Go from your country and your kindred and your father's house to the land that I will show you. And I will make of you a great nation, and I will bless you, and make your name great, so that you will be a blessing. I will bless those who bless you, and him who curses you I will curse; and by you all the families of the earth shall bless themselves."

In this word of blessing is to be found the very essence of the biblical faith. At the very beginning of the "race" Abram, the father, is singled out to be a recipient of God's blessing-power. The text makes clear that this gift is not meant just for Abram and his seed. Rather, Abram is blessed so that ultimately his

9. Johannes Pedersen, *Israel: Its Life and Culture,* 4 vols. (London: Oxford University Press, 1926), 1:182.

*berakah* will become the blessing of all mankind. This is the over-arching theme of the Bible. The history of Israel and of the church is the history of how this blessing was finally made available to the world. So powerful is this blessing that it supersedes even the covenant at Sinai. Israel may be unfaithful and the covenant may be destroyed; yet this blessing lives on. It is the blessing which ties the Testaments together; the hidden thread which unites the people of God in every age.

Just as God chooses for himself a people, so also does he choose a day. God has endowed the Sabbath with a special power which no other day has. It is the power of peace, tranquillity, and re-creation. As we remember God's creation of man and his consequent dignity on the Sabbath so also do we participate in his re-creation and restoration. Sapped strength is renewed; the sense of personal worth worn thin by a week of toil is restored. The Sabbath day is a day when man can "come to himself," recover his self-esteem, and rejoice in God's creation. For the Israelite, then, this was not just a day for solemn cultic exercises. The point of the Sabbath may be theological but it is not particularly "religious." Without this day, the secret of man's blessing is forgotten; his psychic powers, disturbed; his true dignity, destroyed.

In the fourth commandment we find, as in all the other commandments, both the specific command of Yahweh to a specific people, Israel, and the revelation of the way of *'Elohim* for all mankind. The Sabbath is, as it is interpreted here, a peculiarly Israelite institution, but it also contains a blessing for all men, if they would but recognize it. Without a knowledge of Yahweh, however, the joyous meaning of the Sabbath is obliterated. To the *goi'im* the Sabbath appears either as a day of evil portent or as a time of exceeding dullness which must be rejected. The reason why modern men do not recognize the blessing of the Sabbath is that they have forgotten both their own dignity and him who blesses the day.

The word holy, *ḳadoš*, like the word *berakah* is rich in connotative meaning. Undoubtedly Rudolph Otto in his famous work, *Das*

*Heilige,* has done more to restore an appreciative understanding of the idea of "the holy" than anyone else. Although the philosophy and psychology of religion which underlie this work must be considered suspect,[10] he has certainly done much to rescue "the holy" from the moralistic interpretations foisted upon it by generations of interpreters. The sense of the holy, says Otto, is an overwhelming experience of what he calls the numinous, the *mysterium tremendum.* Otto uses many biblical and postbiblical illustrations to explain what he means, but no passage in the Bible illumines the meaning of holiness better than does the sixth chapter of Isaiah. In this chapter Isaiah describes his vision of God, the king, in the temple.

> In the year that King Uzziah died I saw the Lord sitting upon a throne, high and lifted up; and his train filled the temple. Above him stood the seraphim; each had six wings: with two he covered his face, and with two he covered his feet, and with two he flew. And one called to another and said:
> > "Holy, holy, holy is the Lord of hosts;
> > the whole earth is full of his glory."
> And the foundations of the thresholds shook at the voice of him who called, and the house was filled with smoke. And I said: "Woe is me! For I am lost; for I am a man of unclean lips, and I dwell in the midst of a people of unclean lips; for my eyes have seen the King, the Lord of hosts!" (Isaiah 6:1–5).

There are few expressions of the incomprehensible power and majesty and yet proximity of God as compelling as this. Isaiah sees that God is so close that one cannot overlook him; yet he is so unimaginably "lifted up" and mysterious that one cannot begin to comprehend his presence. This is the experience of holiness—an experience of fear and joy, bewilderment and fascination, exalta-

10. Otto, as a Neo-Kantian, tries to ground religious knowledge upon a "numinous category of valuation" which is natural to man and which provides human beings with the possibility of "experiencing" God. All religions, he argues, are based upon this *a priori* category. In his later works, however, he seems implicitly to deny this idea by his observation that the experience of the holy is peculiarly Judeo-Christian and hence is not the ground of all religious experience.

tion and contrition all at once. God is set apart from the world; yet his glory fills the whole earth.

In an ultimate sense, God alone can be holy. To ascribe to objects in this world holiness may be to take a giant step toward idolatry. Still, Israel also knows that though no earthly thing is holy in itself it can be given holiness through the presence of God. Israel is called to be set apart as a holy nation. She is summoned to be distinct from all the other peoples of the world in order that she may be, paradoxically, the locus from which God's glory radiates in the world.

God also sanctifies certain cultic objects. For instance, because of his presence, the ark of the Lord becomes *kadoš*. Thus when Uzzah seeks to prevent the ark from tipping over, he is struck down by its overwhelming power (2 Samuel 6:8). To us this may seem like a piece of ancient superstition, but it need not be regarded as such. After all, Uzzah knew the ark of the covenant to be the seat of God, before whom all men must stand in awe. Although his reflexes caused him to reach out to steady it, his mind and his heart told him that the ark was holy. The shock of what he had done might well have produced a fatal heart attack.

Basically, however, the Israelites were rather unique in their hesitation to think in terms of sanctified space. Even the ark was a movable shrine which could be carried about. To be sure, the Temple later came to be regarded as holy, but this belief was shattered when the Temple was destroyed and the glory of Yahweh departed. For Israel it was not spatial objects but persons and time which God sanctifies.[11] Hence, in the Decalogue it is not a place but a day which God blesses as holy. Not only does he give the Sabbath a blessing; he makes that blessing the power of his own holiness. Thus, although the Sabbath law is a "natural law" providing a breathing space needed by all men, it is also a day when the incomprehensibility and grandeur of *Yahweh 'Elohim* is to be remembered and proclaimed.

11. Abraham J. Heschel, *The Sabbath* (New York: Harper and Row, 1962), pp. 79–83. This book is one of the most beautiful and penetrating works ever written concerning the Sabbath.

## Chapter 9

# MARRIAGE, PARENTHOOD, AND THE COVENANT

"Honor your father and your mother, that your days may be long in the land which the LORD your God gives you."

Like the fourth commandment, this fifth word of the Decalogue can be understood both as a statement of what used to be called "natural law" and as a specific command derived from the exodus. From the first perspective it simply states a truth which most peoples in most countries have recognized: the continued existence of every family, people, nation, and civilization depends to a great extent upon the maintenance of wholesome relations between the generations. Thus, in virtually every society there exists a set of customs, traditions, and commandments designed to strengthen the bond between parents and children and to promote concern for offspring and respect for elders. To be sure, such customs differ considerably from culture to culture and oftentimes seem to be at variance one with another, but at root their purpose is the same. Even the Eskimo sons who, because of the particular conditions of their environment, are expected to slay their fathers when they reach a certain age, believe that they show respect in so doing. For them, to allow their fathers to reach an age when they can no longer hunt or participate in the life of the tribe would be to show dishonor.

There are, of course, those who would argue that all values are relative and that no moral commandments are absolute. In one sense, this may be so, for the specific ways in which basic human problems are dealt with vary from culture to culture. Moral relativists would have a difficult time, however, finding a culture which has existed for long in which filial respect of some sort is not valued.

The whole burden of maintaining the proper relations between generations does not rest upon the sons and daughters. The second commandment has already made clear that it is the older generation which has the primary responsibility, for its sins will be visited upon the children and the children's children. Fathers and mothers must act with the utmost care, lest their sins infect and distort the lives of succeeding generations. Nevertheless, the fourth commandment makes it plain that the younger generation cannot simply blame the elders for its faults. The sins of the fathers may be "visited," but the younger generation also shares the responsibility for evil. Evil sons are not necessarily the result of evil fathers nor are righteous sons necessarily the result of righteous fathers. A perverse father can have a righteous son and a righteous father may discover that, despite his good example and training, his son has become perverse or rebellious.

In any event, the importance of the maintenance of good relations between generations is not a unique discovery made by Israel. Even the most primitive cannibal knows that a special bond exists between parent and child, a bond which must not be casually treated or cavalierly broken. The fifth commandment expresses a truth which mankind in general has learned through long, if sometimes agonizing, experience. Still, the fifth commandment cannot be dismissed as simply a matter of common sense. In order to appreciate the distinctive features of Israel's understanding of the relation between parents and children we must return once more to the first chapters of Genesis to study the teachings offered there concerning marriage, the family, and the image of God.

## PARENTHOOD AND THE IMAGE OF GOD

Genesis 1:26–27 contains a brief description of the creation of man which has long puzzled commentators.

> Then God said, "Let us make man in our image, after our likeness; and let them have dominion over the fish of the sea, and over the birds of the air, and over the cattle, and over all the earth, and over every creeping thing that creeps upon the earth." So God created man in his own image, in the image of God he created him; male and female he created them.

The reason for the scholarly puzzlement is found in the first line. Why does God say "let *us*" and "in *our* image"? Why does he not say "Let me make man in my image"? Various theories have been proposed to answer these questions. Some have found in this usage a trace of polytheism which the author or editor forgot to remove. This explanation, however, does not seem very convincing, for if this passage is exilic or postexilic, as scholars generally agree, there seems little chance that the author would have allowed remnants of polytheism to remain. Whoever wrote this passage clearly chose his words too carefully for that. To think that the author or editor of this passage—which so clearly teaches that the whole world depends completely upon one God for its existence— would have allowed such an obvious remnant of polytheism to remain seems inconceivable.

Nor is the argument that this is a conscious picturing of God as seated upon his throne, surrounded by his legions of angels much more convincing. If this were the case, why is there no mention of the creation and status of these angels? When angels are finally mentioned in Genesis, they appear simply as messengers of God. Any event, object, or person which communicates God's will can be designated an angel, a *malak*. Furthermore, if God is speaking to his angels, man would then be created in the image of angels as well as in the image of God. It is difficult to know what sense to make out of that.

What then does the passage mean? The argument that this is simply a "royal we"—kings often speak in the plural when referring to themselves—would be convincing, if it were not for one fact. Just as the text seems to place emphasis upon both the oneness and the more-than-oneness of God, so also does it place emphasis upon both the oneness and the duality of man. "So God created man in his own image, in the image of God he created him; male and female he created them" (Genesis 1:27). Man *('adam)* is one; yet he is also two: *zakar* and *nekebah,* male and female.[1]

Is not the book of Genesis pointing to both a mystery of man and a mystery of God? The truth about *'adam* is that he is two. Neither male nor female could survive more than one generation alone. For man to continue on the earth, male and female must be united as one flesh. Genesis connects this mystery of man and the image of God very clearly: "In the image of God he created him; male and female he created them" (Genesis 1:27). Does this mean that although God is one, there is within him duality? Does this mean that somehow God, the speaker, and the Spirit of God which moves upon the face of the waters (Genesis 1:2) unite to create the universe? Perhaps this interpretation smacks too much of Trinitarianism to be considered good Old Testament exegesis. Still, the text does seem to point toward a mystery in God which is mirrored in man's duality. Just as God creates, so man procreates.[2] His *berakah* is to be able to be fruitful and multiply and fill the earth and subdue it.

In the merely biological act of sexual intercourse, man fulfills a function common to the animals and therefore may not seem to

1. The word *zakar* is etymologically related to the Hebrew word meaning to remember. Doubtless the male is so designated because he bears the names of his forefathers and hence is the bearer of the family's remembrance. The word *nekebah* is derived from *nakab,* to pierce or perforate and hence describes woman's biological role as "the penetrated."

2. Nicholas of Cusa, among others, argues that the doctrine of creation necessitates a Trinitarian position. Nicholas Cusanus, *Of Learned Ignorance,* trans. Fr. Germain Heron (London: Routledge and Kegan Paul, 1954), pp. 89–92.

mirror God's image. For man, however, procreation is never merely biological. In the physical act man enters not only union but communion. At its best, love is always more than desire; the family, more than an association of convenience. In man, therefore, the sex act is transformed and transcended. Just as God creates the world, so man, his vice-regent, creates his own world, the family.

In the second chapter of Genesis the relation between man and woman is described somewhat differently, but the essential idea is the same. In this version of man's creation, *'adam* (man) is created one; he is male and female together. In fact, Adam, as he is created, should not be called "he" but rather "he-she." In this state man is lonesome and therefore looks for a companion but finds none. Although Adam names the animals and creates thereby a personally ordered world, no fit companion is found. God, therefore, has compassion for Adam and causes a deep sleep to fall upon him-her. Then, from Adam's body he takes a "rib" or "side" and fashions a suitable helpmate.

Scripture uses language very carefully at this point. It is important to notice that after the creation of woman, the male is not called *'adam* but *iš,* while the woman is called *iššah. 'Adam* is not the male but *iš* and *iššah* joined together as one flesh. Only after the act of disobedience does the male begin to call himself Adam and in turn call his wife *Ḥawah,* or as the Greek has it, Eve. It is inappropriate, then, to speak of Adam and Eve in paradise. When the male begins to express his arrogance by claiming for himself complete humanity, paradise is already forsaken.

Skeptics have, for centuries, made fun of Adam's rib and the highly unscientific nature of the story. Even biblical scholars have pronounced the writer of Genesis 2 and 3 as primitive and naive.[3] Nothing could be further from the truth. That this is not meant to be a scientific account of the creation of man is made clear by a

3. Fleming James, *Personalities of the Old Testament* (New York: Charles Scribner's Sons, 1951), p. 197. James describes the "Yahwist's" writings as "crudely anthropomorphic," "primitive," and "naive," but argues that these traits are a result of his dependence upon an older material.

number of features in the story itself[4] and by the fact that it is placed side by side with another account of creation which disagrees with it about a number of factual details. Instead of being primitive, this myth is a very sophisticated attempt to describe, among other things, the nature of sexuality, marriage, and the family as man experiences them. In essence, it is a radical endorsement of the value of heterosexual relations and as such distinguishes the biblical tradition from most other religions.

Socrates may have married Xantippe and, in fact, may have loved her, but when he searched for the truth, she was left behind. Gautama Buddha too was married, but to find the peace he desired he felt compelled to leave his family and his goods to sit under a Bo tree. Even the Canaanites who made sexuality and the fertility rites the center of their religion negated the highest meaning of sexuality by using it for ulterior reason—to engender fertility in the soil. For Israel, on the other hand, marriage is not just a relationship which one enters into to satisfy desires or produce rain for crops. Neither is it one of the shackles of the world from which wise men seek release. For Israel, marriage is the reconstitution of *'adam,* the fulfillment of both male and female and the reflection of God's image. The male may call himself *'adam,* but he deceives himself. He is but a fragment of *'adam* without the female. Nor can the woman find completion for herself without the male. Outside of marriage she remains but half a person. For this reason eunuchs were rejected from Israel and homosexuals were condemned. The rabbis even argued seriously for centuries concerning whether an unmarried man could be considered a full-fledged member of the household of Israel. One may well question whether these rabbis did not carry this position too far in the sometimes absolute rejection of the unmarried state. The essential position, however, need not be disputed. Marriage is not only justified but extolled. Through marriage male and female become one flesh and as one flesh con-

4. The description of the four rivers flowing from one source outside of Eden indicates that the author is speaking "mythologically." Any well-informed Hebrew would have known that the Tigris and Euphrates, to say nothing of the Nile, do not flow from one common source.

stitute *'adam,* the image of God. As God creates, so this *'adam* procreates. As God treats his creation with fatherly care, so father and mother watch over, provide for, and nourish their children.

The father and mother are, therefore, the reflection of God's creative and sustaining power to their children. If a child is to know *Yahweh 'Elohim* he will doubtless first be confronted by him through his human reflection. Thus children are called to honor their parents, for it is through them that God's glory is made manifest.

The word "honor" is a translation of *kabod,* a Hebrew word which means, in the first instance, "to be heavy." This commandment, then, could well be translated, "Give weight to your father and mother." That is to say, let your parents have influence in your lives. When God is said to have glory in the world what is meant is that he has "weight" or influence. Like a force which presses down at a particular point so that the pressure radiates over the whole surface, so is God's glory in the world. God presses down upon Israel and the whole world feels his influence. Just as God has glory in the world, so are parents to have glory among their children. Sons and daughters are to acknowledge and respond to the glory in their lives which parents already exert.

Significantly, the word "honor" rather than the word "obey" is used to express a child's proper attitude toward his parents. Children are expected to respond positively to their parents' influence, but this does not mean that they must always agree with them. This commandment is no invitation to parental tyranny. Though children should certainly not rebel at the least whim and are expected to listen carefully to their parents, they are left with a certain amount of freedom. They owe their parents respect, but not servitude. Thus there developed in Israel no deification of ancestors such as was found in China nor any tradition of absolute obedience to the elderly.

It is also interesting that rabbinical commentaries, by and large, do not stress so much doing what father and mother command as caring for their needs when they are unable to care for themselves.

In general, this commandment is taken to apply primarily to adults who have elderly parents and is interpreted as meaning that sons and daughters should care for their elders.

> Support your parents generously; support them even if you have to go a-begging (Kiddushin et al.). A man who can afford it and does not support his aged parents is a murderer. God is bitterly disappointed in such a man. "I made respect of them of equal importance with respect of Me," He thunders against him.[5]

Jesus makes the same point when he criticizes the Pharisees for claiming to uphold the Law while finding loopholes in it so that they can avoid supporting their parents (Mark 7:10–13).

## MARRIAGE AND THE COVENANT

Throughout this whole discussion one question of great importance has been left unasked: How is this commandment related to the word spoken to Israel in the exodus? Is this simply a practical law tacked onto the covenant or is it integrally related to the word-event of salvation? To answer this question we must return again to the story of Adam. Although *iš* and *iššah* are seen to be "meant for each other"—*iššah* is bone of *iš's* bone and flesh of his flesh—Genesis also makes clear that somehow this naturally harmonious relation has been disrupted. Because mankind has learned to make value judgments concerning God's good creation, man and woman have become mutually suspicious and envious. As soon as the fruit of the tree of the knowledge of good and evil is eaten, both male and female become ashamed of their genitals and seek to cover them. The woman senses a biologically subservient role and finds her great glory, the ability to bear children, a curse. The male, on the other hand, sees in the woman the source of his discontent and blames her for their problem. His accusation, "The woman whom thou gavest to be with me, she gave me fruit of the tree, and I ate" (Genesis 3:12), expresses the male's perennial

5. Solomon Goldman, *The Ten Commandments,* ed. Maurice Samuel (Chicago: University of Chicago Press, 1956), p. 178.

attitude toward his helpmate. As a result of disobedience, what was meant to be a harmonious reflection of the image of God becomes a seething caldron of discontent and ill will. Although male and female know that they cannot exist independently, they find it almost equally difficult to exist together. This, according to Genesis 3, is the paradoxical position in which men and women find themselves.

With the covenant, however, Israel and God are reconciled. When Israel truly hears God's voice, disobedience is turned to obedience; hate and fear are turned to love. Because Israel is made right with God through his act of manumission and salvation, she is made right with all of the conflicting forces of existence. Reconciliation with God implies reconciliation between man and woman as well.[6]

Not only does God call man and woman to be reconciled one with another through his word-event; he also provides a prototype in his marriage to Israel, according to which human marriage should be patterned. Male is to be to female as Yahweh is to Israel, and vice versa. In one sense, of course, the description of the covenant as a marriage is a metaphor drawn from human experience. We liken God's relation to Israel to a man's relation to his wife. Still, this covenant provides a prototype of what human relations should be like. Henceforth, when Israel speaks of human marriage she must speak metaphorically, using the covenant as the anchor for her symbolic language.

Many of the prophets use the same imagery, only in a negative way. Jeremiah, for instance, says that in the present age the merrymaking of the bridegroom and the bride is stilled because the covenant is broken, but that in the new age, when the new covenant is made, the bridegroom and the bride again will rejoice.[7] In other words, human marriages reflect the state of the divine-

6. It is interesting that the Hebrew word for marriage means also "sanctification." It might be fruitful to explore the possibility of developing a doctrine of sanctification based upon the biblical understanding of marriage.

7. Jeremiah 16:9; 31:4, 13, 31–34.

human marriage. When Israel's knowledge and love of Yahweh is firm and strong, human marriages are firm and strong, but when Israel goes astray, human marriages lose their permanence.[8]

In summary, God, through his covenant with Israel at Sinai, calls children to honor their fathers and mothers, for through the covenant father and mother are reconciled and thus reflect the image of God. Marriage and parenthood can again be given the value accorded them at creation, for when Israel hears God's voice heterosexual animosity is overcome. In honoring the father the child honors the reflection of God himself who can now be addressed as Father. In honoring the mother, the child honors Israel, God's chosen bride, the vessel of his Holy Spirit. It is interesting that in Judaism even today, though the father is the religious head of the household,[9] membership in the household of Israel passes through the mother. A child with a Jewish mother is regarded as Jewish, no matter what the religion of the father may be.

Such teaching regarding the reconciliation of man and woman through the covenant can, of course, be taken to foolish extremes. Obviously there is nothing magical about the covenant, for even the most faithful Israelite has marital problems now and then. Still, it is a striking fact that among Israelites marriage and family ties have been and are particularly strong. For many Jews the essence of their religion is found not in the synagogue but in the family rituals in the home. There is, perhaps, no better expression of the reconciliation of the sexes than the seder service at Passover in which father and mother play their complementary roles. The voice of the father may dominate, but it is the mother who lights the candles and who leads in the responses. Here we see in human form an image of that covenant between Yahweh and Israel con-

8. It may be significant that by the time of Jesus, Jewish marriages were anything but permanent. Divorce was, for the husband at least, very easy to obtain.

9. As a matter of fact, in strictly orthodox Judaism it is the man who attends synagogue services. The wife need not attend or, if she does so, occupies a segregated area, usually in the rear.

summated at Sinai. It is a living sign that God's covenant with Israel is still a reality.

## "THAT YOUR DAYS MAY BE LONG"

Like many other peoples of the world Israel valued her existence upon the earth and considered a long life a blessing. This emphasis upon the importance of life here and now was greatly underlined by the fact that during most of her existence Israel accepted no belief in personal existence after death. To be sure, writings from the postexilic age do hint that death is not a final end, but these are only hints.[10] On the whole, Israel refused to accept any comforting doctrine of individual immortality. Man is finite. He is created by God at conception and when death comes, he, for all intents and purposes, simply ceases to exist.

The Bible does, of course, speak of *Šeol*, that shadowy pit where the *nepeš* (that is, life) goes after death, but one cannot think of life in *Šeol* as in any way constituting individual immortality. Life continues to exist there, but in an indiscriminate and virtually unconscious way. *Kohelet* expresses well the Hebraic vision of *Šeol* when he writes:

> A living dog is better than a dead lion. For the living know that they will die, but the dead know nothing, and they have no more reward; but the memory of them is lost. Their love and their hate and their envy have already perished, and they have no more for ever any share in all that is done under the sun. . . . Whatever your hand finds to do, do it with your might; for there is no work or thought or knowledge or wisdom in *Šeol*, to which you are going (Ecclesiastes 9:4-6, 10).

*Šeol* then is a way of explaining where life, which appears real enough, goes when death comes, but it provides no comfort or peace. This life is all man has; he should look forward to no heavenly rewards in the future, according to the Old Testament.

Israel's refusal to develop a belief in immortality cannot be con-

10. The clearest assertions of a belief in the resurrection are to be found in Isaiah 26:19 and in Daniel 12:2.

ceived as simply a matter of ignorance or primitive naiveté, for she doubtless knew all about the Egyptian ideas of immortality and their profound effect upon that culture, but consciously rejected them as being an expression of man's sin. In the story of Adam in Genesis 3 no word is said about man's immortality until after man has eaten of the tree of the knowledge of good and evil. Then man's eyes are opened and he sees as a curse the fact that he is created out of the dust of the earth (Genesis 3:19). Now, man begins to yearn for immortality, but God refuses it to him (Genesis 3:22–24). Christian theologians have often interpreted this passage to mean that although man was created to be immortal, he lost his immortality through disobedience. The text, however, belies this interpretation. Man is created from the dust of the earth and therefore is finite, physical, and mortal. To be sure, God breathes into him the breath of life and he becomes a living being, a *nepeš*, but a *nepeš* is by no means an immortal substance. *Nepeš* simply means life and this life cannot be separated from the physical body. Animals have *nepešot* too; man is not unique in this respect.[11]

The problem with man is not that he has lost his immortality but rather that he has gained the propensity to judge the world and therefore can no longer accept his finitude. He yearns for the tree of life—which he did not desire before his disobedience—but he cannot reach it. God has placed a flaming sword in his path so that he can never return to Eden and the tree. The implication is, however, that if man could really return to his state of innocence he would no longer desire the tree of life because he would no longer consider finitude and mortality evil.

Israel, therefore, refused to accept the notions of life beyond the grave so common among her neighbors. Eventually, however, a belief in existence and meaning beyond this life did develop. This occurred when the continuation of Israel as a corporate body seemed threatened during and after her years in exile. When Israel spoke of life after death she did so in a characteristically

11. Johannes Pedersen, *Israel: Its Life and Culture,* 4 vols. (London: Oxford University Press, 1926), 1:100.

Hebraic fashion. What she emphasized was not the immortality of the soul, which is quite incomprehensible in terms of "biblical psychology," but the resurrection of the body. This concept retains all the truth of the doctrine of man's mortality so emphasized throughout the Old Testament; yet it also provides meaning for this seemingly unjust life. According to this doctrine, man is finite and when he dies, is dead. There is no immortal substance hidden within him. Man's hope rests not in himself but in God alone, for his hope is not in his own personal continuation but in God who will re-create him, body and soul together. The idea of the resurrection of the body places man's trust totally and completely in God. It is he alone who can give hope for existence beyond death. This existence will not be in some soul-inhabited heaven, but in a new earth created by God and inhabited by men and women with real bodies.

As has already been said, however, the development of this doctrine came quite late in the history of Israel. Until the time of the exile, Israelites placed their hopes, not in the future of the self, but in the continuation of the family and the people. The individual found meaning in the fact that just as he bore his father's name, so his son would bear his. Not only did Israel (Jacob) father twelve sons, those twelve sons were Israel, they were a part of his body. Through procreation Israel became a people; even today the patriarch lives in his sons and daughters.

This truth is symbolized in the name which a son bears. Although that name is usually shortened to, for instance, Jesus Bar-Joseph, the full name is really equivalent to his full genealogy. Since the name is, in fact, the denotation of the existence of a person, all of these ancestors live in the offspring. Thus the son is, in a concrete physical sense, not only the continuation of his father but also of all the fathers who have gone before. Through him the name, and thus the identity of the forefathers, is preserved.

This belief makes the fourth commandment particularly important, for when a son fails to honor his father he really dishonors the whole line of ancestors stretching from the beginning to the present, for his father is, in fact, the embodiment of all of those ancestors. Furthermore, he risks the possibility that his son will in turn dishonor him, for he no longer bears the family names honorably. When this happens his name is blotted out and remembered no more.

## "IN THE LAND WHICH THE LORD YOUR GOD GIVES YOU"

The word 'adamah, which means land, indicates how intimately related man and the land were thought to be. Just as *iš* and *iššah* belong together, so also 'adam and 'adamah are meant to be united, for the land is the psychic counterpart of man. Man is commanded to till the garden and keep it; he is meant to dominate the earth. In Eden 'adam and 'adamah were like husband and wife, living together in mutual harmony.

Through man's act of disobedience, however, this harmony was destroyed. Man came to regard his agricultural labors a curse. He resented the fact that he had been taken from the dust of the 'adamah and must return to 'adamah at death. Adam was allowed to continue his tilling of the soil outside of the garden, but now his relation to the soil was one of struggle and frustration. Cain, in fact, could not believe that the fruits of his labors were acceptable to God. Only when, as a result of his murder of Abel, Cain was made a wanderer upon the earth, did he appreciate how much man needs the land for self-fulfillment, security, and psychic well-being (Genesis 4:13–14). Like the male's relation to the female, man's relation to the land is two-sided. On the one hand, the 'adamah is a source of backbreaking work which man continually wishes to escape. On the other, the 'adamah is a source of meaning and security which man desperately needs .Therefore, man's life is lived in constant but ambivalent tension with the land. He would like to become a traveler who need not work; yet he knows that perpetual wandering is a dreadful curse. What man needs, therefore, is some way through which he can become reconciled with the land and with work which the land demands of him.

One of the predominant themes of the Torah is God's promise and subsequent gift of a land to his people. Through the conquest, Israel, the wanderer, becomes the people of the land. With this event, man's reconciliation with his environment is complete. Of course, as a matter of fact, the conquest (and hence the reconciliation) was never total. The Canaanites and other original inhabitants remained in the land and continued as both a political and spiritual threat to Israel. Still, at least a partial restoration of Israel's natural relation to the land occurred. The Book of Joshua recounts how the land was conquered and then parcelled out, first according to tribe and then according to family. Each family received an inheritance which was to be preserved as long as the family remained. This property could, of course, be bought and sold, but with the provision that the family inheritance would be restored at the year of Jubilee, that is, every fifty years.[12] Thus 'adam, in effect, was again married to 'adamah.

The seriousness with which this reconciliation of man and the land was taken is well illustrated in both the Law and Prophets. Among the twelve curses pronounced in Deuteronomy 27 is a curse uttered against him "who removes his neighbor's landmark" (Deuteronomy 27:17). The importance of this curse against anyone who alters the extent of some neighbor's family inheritance is underlined by the fact that only the most serious sort of moral offenses is included in this list. Another illustration is found in the story of Naboth and his vineyard (1 Kings 21). Naboth, a private citizen, owned, as a part of his inheritance, a vineyard which King Ahab very much desired. Ahab asked to buy it, but Naboth refused to sell. As a result, Jezebel, Ahab's pagan queen, engineered the death of Naboth and then simply confiscated Naboth's land. This exercise of royal power in violation of the rights of inheritance not only produced a strong protest on the part of Elijah; according to Scripture it also led to the ultimate downfall of the house of Omri. Because of his contrition, Ahab's life, for the time being, was

12. Leviticus 25:8–17.

173

spared, but his son Joram was killed by the revolutionary Jehu who, with poetic justice, buried him in Naboth's plot (2 Kings 9:26).

## "WHICH THE LORD YOUR GOD GIVES YOU"

The use of the participle, *noten*, rather than either a perfect or imperfect form of *natan*, "to give," indicates that God did not just give the land once and for all to Israel. Rather, God's gift of the land is always happening and depends upon Israel's obedience to the covenant. When the covenant is broken, when father and mother are not honored, the family and the nation risk severing the restored bond between *'adam* and *'adamah*. Although the commandment does not say that every son who fails to honor his father and mother will be disinherited, it implies that this may well happen. In this case, the son is separated from his land and must become a wanderer upon the earth.

When Israel as a whole fails to abide by the covenant, she too risks similar, tragic consequences. Prophets such as Amos and Hosea saw that this would, in fact, be the result of their people's disobedience. The exile imposed upon Israel first by Assyria and then by Babylonia was more than just a painful uprooting of a large segment of the population. It was a sign that the reconciliation of *'adam* and *'adamah* had been destroyed and that, therefore, the reconciliation wrought through the covenant was destroyed as well.

The people of Judah, of course, were allowed to return to their land by the Persians, and at least some of them did so. Thus the separation was partially overcome. In A.D. 70, however, the Romans again destroyed Jerusalem and much of Jewish Palestine was depopulated. From that time until the twentieth century, the old Israel has been a people without a land. Jacob, the traveler, became once more the wandering Jew. Is the establishment of the nation of Israel in our time a sign that God's reconciling power is again at work among his people? Is this an eschatological portent of a new era at hand? We must wait and see.

174

Chapter 10

# THE LIMITATIONS AND
# DEMANDS OF FREEDOM

Above all else, the word which God speaks at Sinai is a word of freedom. Through this *dabar* Israel is delivered from the false and degrading enslavement to the gods of this world so that she may love Yahweh, the God who "brings out," and participate in his reconciling covenant. The exodus event calls Israel to recognize the dignity and freedom which Yahweh bestows upon her and upon all mankind and to commit herself to this freedom. She is summoned to rejoice in her earthly existence—in work and creativity, in sexuality and familial life—for this life is given to man not as a curse, but as a blessing.

Commitment to the God who frees and reconciles and to the consequent freedom and reconciliation involves responsibility. He who hears the "I" of Yahweh can no longer do as he pleases, for the recognition of this voice inevitably places certain limitations upon what one can do to others and constitutes an absolute demand to work for the well-being of others. Not only is man called to "be himself" and hence to delight in his own creativity and procreativity; he is also warned that he must take care lest he violate the dignity of others. Thus the hearer of this word is, as Luther would have it, both "a perfectly free lord of all, subject to none" and "a perfectly dutiful servant of all, subject to all."[1]

1. Martin Luther, "The Freedom of a Christian," trans. W. A. Lambert, rev. by Harold J. Grimm in *Three Treatises* (Philadelphia: Fortress Press, 1960), p. 277; also in Luther's Works, vol. 31 (Philadelphia: Fortress Press, 1957), p. 344.

The last five commandments are based upon this central call to freedom, for they spell out the limitations placed upon an individual's freedom by the recognition of the dignity of other men. They are stated negatively in order to give individuals the maximum amount of freedom while, at the same time, determining the limits beyond which the expression of that freedom must not go.

Our task in this chapter is manifold. We must analyze precisely what the limitations placed upon the expression of man's freedom by these commandments really are, describe how they are further elaborated and qualified in other sections of the Torah, examine more fully the positive commitment to the dignity of man which undergirds them, and in their light analyze some of the pressing moral issues which confront modern men today. This discussion can, of course, be by no means exhaustive, but it is hoped that through this analysis of these last five commandments some of the ethical implications of the Decalogue may become clearer.

### "YOU SHALL NOT KILL"

Although this is the traditional English translation of the sixth commandment, it would be far more accurate to translate it "you shall not murder," for the word *raṣaḥ* which is used here does not denote all types of killing but only premeditated slaying. The Hebrew language is quite rich in words denoting the taking of life. Had a broader meaning been intended the word *harag* would probably have been used. *Raṣaḥ* was undoubtedly chosen because only murder was meant to be prohibited.

The prohibition of murder was not, of course, an innovation of Israel. One can hardly envision a society in which homicide in all forms is allowed; even in primitive cannibalistic communities homicide within the tribe is generally forbidden. No society could exist stably for very long if one person could take another's life in good conscience and without fear of reprisal. Thus, this commandment finds many parallels in nonbiblical codes of law.

Scripture recognizes this fact by making homicide the first crime perpetrated by Adam's children (Genesis 4:8–16) and by placing God's official prohibition of it at the time of Noah (Genesis 9:6). This law, along with the prohibition of the eating of the blood of animals, forms the stipulated basis of God's covenant with Noah and hence with all mankind.

The usual means by which this law was enforced in ancient societies was through the practice of blood revenge. If someone were killed, it was the responsibility of his kinsmen to avenge his death by the death of the killer. Often this began a whole series of deaths as each family retaliated in kind. The power of and horrible problems raised by this tradition are revealed very clearly in Aeschylus' Oresteian trilogy.[2] Orestes is, according to this ancient law, required to kill his mother because she, to avenge her daughter's death, murdered his father. The pendulum of guilt and revenge swings back and forth through the generations; finally it is stopped in a typically Greek fashion, by an appeal to Athena, the goddess of wisdom.

The Torah faces many of the same problems raised in this trilogy, but attempts to solve them in a typically Hebraic fashion. The Old Testament is often deprecated for teaching the vicious law of revenge, "An eye for an eye and a tooth for a tooth,"[3] but it must be recognized that this was undoubtedly a law already in force among Israelites long before they met at Sinai. It was, indeed, a law of the ancient, particularly bedouin, world in general. The Torah accepts it, but then seeks to modify it in a number of crucial ways.

One of the most vexing features of this ancient *lex talionis* was its lack of regard for intentionality. If a man happened by accident to strike and kill another person with his loose axe head, he could expect that he would in turn meet his death at the hands of a blood avenger. He who shed the lifeblood of another, no matter what

2. *Agammemnon,* the first of the three tragedies, presupposes a long history of guilt and revenge which had plagued the house of Atreus. The trilogy itself focuses upon the denouement of this bloody story. For an excellent, readable translation see: Aeschylus, *The Oresteian Trilogy,* trans. Philip Vellacott (Baltimore: Penguin Books, 1956).

3. Exodus 21:24.

the way or reason, would, unless extraordinarily fortunate, meet his death at the hands of man. The Torah does not deny the blood avenger's duty to punish the guilty man, even though the act of homicide was committed without malice aforethought, but it does provide cities of refuge to which the pursued man can flee to find safety (Numbers 35:9–15). Numbers proceeds to specify the general criteria for distinguishing between intentional and unintentional homicide.

> But if he stabbed him suddenly without enmity, or hurled anything on him without lying in wait, or used a stone, by which a man may die, and without seeing him cast it upon him, so that he died, though he was not his enemy, and did not seek his harm; then the congregation shall judge between the manslayer and the avenger of blood, in accordance with these ordinances; and the congregation shall rescue the manslayer from the hand of the avenger of blood, and the congregation shall restore him to his city of refuge, to which he had fled, and he shall live in it until the death of the high priest who was anointed with the holy oil
> (Numbers 35:22–25).

This may not seem like a wholly adequate way of distinguishing accidental death from murder nor like a wholly equitable solution for an innocent man who may have to spend many years in the city of refuge. Outside of that city his life was still in danger and this seems woefully unjust. Still, this was undoubtedly as much of an alteration of the old law of revenge as was possible. Although by modern standards inadequate, this law does at least provide some method of averting the death of a man who has committed murder by accident.

Now, through this law, the *'ēdah,* a congregation-tribunal composed, in all probability, of the male adults of a given community,[4] is placed between the blood avenger and the accused. Although the law of blood revenge remains, it is severely qualified and is sub-

4. The precise nature of the *'ēdah* is not defined in Scripture nor is the relation between the *'ēdah* and the *qahal* fully clarified. For a good, brief discussion see: M. H. Pope, "Congregation, Assembly," in *The Interpreter's Dictionary of the Bible,* 4 vols., ed. G. A. Buttrick et al. (New York: Abingdon Press, 1962), 1:669–70.

jected to the rule and decision of the congregation. This was a major development in the history of jurisprudence which must not be underestimated. Just when this step took place is difficult to ascertain. Since passages concerning the cities of refuge are to be found in virtually every strata of the tradition found in the Torah, it is likely that at least the idea of cities of refuge developed quite early.

## *Murder and Man's Dignity*

Thus far we have been dealing with homicide as it was treated legislatively in the Torah. We must also ask, however, whether this commandment does not have any broader significance than simply a prohibition against homicide. Did Jesus, for instance, legitimately see in this commandment a far more comprehensive meaning or did he propound an essentially new law when he said,

> You have heard that it was said to the men of old, 'You shall not kill; and whoever kills shall be liable to judgment.' But I say to you that every one who is angry with his brother shall be liable to judgment; whoever insults his brother shall be liable to the council, and whoever says, 'You fool!' shall be liable to the hell of fire (Matthew 5:21–22).

Although the limited meaning of *raṣaḥ* seems to imply that any broader application of this sixth commandment is illegitimate, if one begins with the idea that this commandment flows out of the basic faith in the dignity of man already emphasized by the first commandments, what Jesus says seems quite comprehensible. Is he not teaching that ultimately, if one believes that man is made in the image of God, any deprecation of his dignity is forbidden? Is he not using the sixth commandment as a negative corollary of the very positive biblical affirmation of man's value and importance?

If this is so, is it possible to limit this commandment to a prohibition of only homicide? Is not Campbell Morgan correct when he writes:

179

This at once marks as murder the intentional taking of human life, whether by the individual, by the society, or by the nation; and brands as a breaking of the commandment the act of killing, capital punishment, and all war, save where such act, such punishment, such war, immediately and unequivocally follow the clearly-expressed commandment of God.[5]

Morgan argues that in ancient Israel capital punishment was only used when God's law expressly required it and that wars were fought successfully by Israel only when God clearly commanded them. Hence, he concludes that modern Christians must take the same point of view and must eschew war except when God directly commands. Since, we might add, God's commands are seldom clearly expressed today in regard to war, Morgan seems to be saying that no Christian can countenance war. Must a Christian then be a pacifist?

## *War*

It must be recognized first that nowhere in the Bible is the waging of or participation in war forbidden. Throughout her history, Israel was involved in armed conflict against her neighbors. Nor were these wars always specifically commanded by God, as Morgan says. Insofar as God was in charge of all events, he indeed called Israel into battle, but there was only rarely a special revelation or call to a holy war. God called Israel to fight primarily through the impulse for self-preservation. Thus there seems to be no legalistic reason to forbid war.

When one looks at the spirit of the law, however, there may be more reason to hesitate. If one regards all other men as created in the image of God, can human blood be shed under any circumstances? Are there any times when a believer can legitimately take up arms and shoot to kill? It is sometimes argued that with the coming of Christ the new Israel was freed from the old law and therefore a legalistic answer to such a question is insufficient. Still, the Christian is not freed from basic belief in the dignity of man.

5. G. Campbell Morgan, *The Ten Commandments* (New York: Fleming H. Revell Co., 1901), p. 68.

He cannot escape by saying that "all is forgiven," for Jesus did away with the legalistic accretions to the law, not to make God's word less demanding but in order that Israel might see more clearly the absolute claims of the spirit of the law.

Because Jesus abolishes *do ut des* legalism, however, no legalistic answer can be propounded by a Christian as Morgan tries to do. Rather, the Christian must ask at every step upon his way, is what I am doing consistent with my obedience to God and with my recognition of the dignity of all men? Sometimes a Christian must conclude that participation in war is the only way open which seems to preserve human dignity. Frequently, however, he must conclude that it does not. Sometimes a war is waged for the cause of justice, but one may well doubt that there ever has been such a thing as a "holy war." When a nation begins to point to its "just cause" as a mandate from heaven, the Christian must beware, for more often than not just causes heralded by a nation are simply a cloak for aggrandizement.

Nevertheless, there can be no one Christian answer to the question of war. In every age the church, and each individual Christian, must rethink the question in terms of the particular situation. The answers which were given to justify the war against Hitler may not be at all appropriate when confronted by the war against the Viet Cong. Men who willingly fought in one war may become, with equal willingness, conscientious objectors in the next. A Christian must neither become so idealistic that he fails to support the cause of justice nor so realistic that he fails to protest injustice. The Christian who participates personally in a war must do so with the clear recognition that he involves himself in guilt by so doing. Even in the most just war, killing is killing. On the other hand, the Christian who refuses to participate in a war must not assume that he has, thereby, avoided all guilt. He must recognize that whether he likes it or not he shares the guilt of his whole nation by his very existence in it. Furthermore, he must stand responsible for the injustice which may arise because his nation has not battled keenly enough for the cause of justice.

In conclusion, then, it must be said that the Christian need not be and, in fact, should not be a pacifist "by definition." In every situation, he must attempt to hear what the word of God calls him to do. Thus, although he may not accept pacifism as a general policy, he may well choose to be a pacifist in a particular situation. In any case, he must recognize his own involvement in the guilt of mankind, and rely not upon his righteousness, but upon the forgiveness of God.[6]

## Capital Punishment

The question of capital punishment is also a complicated one. From a legalistic point of view, a believer in Scripture can accept this form of punishment, for the Torah countenances, indeed demands, capital punishment for a number of offenses such as murder and adultery. In fact, however, our modern sensibilities are sometimes repelled by the imposition of the death penalty demanded by the Torah, for both blasphemy and youthful rebellion are regarded as punishable by death.[7]

Still, if one regards the question from the point of view of a belief in human dignity, the whole issue becomes more complicated. It may be, of course, that at the time(s) when the legal precedents of the Torah were formulated, capital punishment was an absolute necessity. The denial of such a punishment would doubtless have meant not better justice, but a return to older

6. The fact that the believer is often caught in ambiguous moral situations in which no action seems absolutely justifiable indicates the weakness of both legalistic ethics and the type of situational ethic which emphasizes love alone as the basis for ethical decisions. (Cf. Joseph Fletcher, *Situation Ethics* [Philadelphia: Westminster Press, 1966].) Legalism surely cannot always account for the complexity of man's moral dilemmas, but a simple appeal to love doesn't always help either. For instance, a man may fight for his country with the belief that, on the whole, he is fighting for justice in the world. Nevertheless, he can hardly say, as he shoots an enemy soldier, "I am doing this because I love you." Reinhold Niebuhr's analysis of the human predicament is, I believe, very cogent at this point. A man may wage war for the sake of justice, but his own conscience tells him that even if the ultimate goal is good, he still stands in need of God's forgiveness for using the means which he does to reach that goal. The Old Covenant of obedience, therefore, points forward to the New Covenant of forgiveness.

7. Leviticus 24:16; Deuteronomy 21:18–21.

tribal patterns of revenge. The question we must ask is, do the reasons for the use of capital punishment during the biblical period still exist? And further, does this form of punishment accomplish what it sets out to do? Does it really act as a deterrant for future crimes? Is it the only recourse by which a society can be preserved and individuals protected? In other words, does it promote the well-being of society and the individuals in it?

These are questions which must be answered, in part, by the sociologist. The tentative results of sociological research seem to support the claim that capital punishment no longer functions as an effective deterrant.[8] Furthermore, there is evidence that at least some murderers can be reoriented and redeemed so that they can live good, useful lives. Therefore, it is quite conceivable that capital punishment may best be abolished.

Such a conclusion should not, however, be based upon a legalistic reading of the sixth commandment. The sixth commandment may tell us that it is wrong to murder, but it does not deny capital punishment. What the Christian must look for is the best deterrant for crime and the best way to organize society so that criminals do not develop. If capital punishment seems the best deterrant, then we are free to use it, though with extreme caution. If not, we are compelled to look for other methods by which to prevent and remedy the complex social and moral conditions which produce criminals. Above all, we must endeavor to build a society in which the dignity of men is emphasized and the lives of individuals protected.

## Induced Abortion

The question of induced abortion is again a very complicated problem which has been a storm center for dispute for centuries. One of the basic questions is: Is an undeveloped embryo a person? Is the destruction of such an embryo murder? All kinds of casuistical lines can be drawn to prove one point or another. One could argue that because an embryo is not yet born, it cannot act so as to

8. John Drinkwater, "Capital Punishment? No." in *Capital Punishment,* ed. Grant S. McClellan (New York: H. W. Wilson Co., 1961), p. 34.

reflect the image of God and therefore to destroy it is not murder. An equally good case could be made for the position that once an embryo is "quick" it is a person and therefore has a right, under the Providence of God, to life.[9] If an embryo can be destroyed, why not a newborn baby?

The first point to be made in answer to these questions, is that no legalistic answer can be given on the basis of Scripture. Neither in the Old nor the New Testaments is the appropriateness or even the possibility of abortion considered. Surely, however, both the prohibition of murder and the positive assertion of the dignity of man point to the conclusion that acts of premeditated abortion must not be taken lightly.[10] They must not be performed simply for the convenience of the mother or the family or the state. God grants life and therefore life is of value and must be preserved if possible. At the same time, when the health or life of the mother is at stake there may be instances when a premeditated abortion is the lesser of two evils. The Christian should first of all attempt through the methods now available to prevent unwanted or harmful pregnancies. Preventative measures of birth control are less harmful and surely much safer than induced abortion.[11] If conception does occur, however, the Christian must, in good conscience, decide the case on its own merits. He may approve of abortion in some instances as the lesser of two evils, but must also understand that even in this situation abortion is still evil. As in the case of war, abortion is never good, but the alternatives may be worse.

### Suicide

Are there any times when the premeditated killing of oneself is justified? The usual Christian answer to this question seems to

9. The idea of an embryo being "quick" is now, I understand, somewhat out-of-date biologically. This does not totally destroy the strength of the argument, however.
10. Acts of premeditated abortion, of course, include not only "operations" but also the use of drugs, exercise, and other means to produce a miscarriage.
11. Infra., pp. 190–193.

be, "No, the taking of one's own life is a sin against God." Only God has the right to take away life. Although this general conclusion seems to be implied by the sixth commandment, there may be special circumstances in which suicide, in one form or another, is not only justified but an expression of obedience to God.

Surely, most instances of suicide are examples of lack of faith in God and in the value of man. They are expressions of hopelessness and guilt which the word of God, when heard, overcomes. Nevertheless, Jesus is reported to have said that "Greater love has no man than this, that a man lay down his life for his friends" (John 15:13). Furthermore, he himself reveals what true "suicide" is by waiting in the Garden of Gethsemane for his enemies to come. He probably could have escaped easily, had he so desired. He probably could have saved himself even after having been captured by answering his questioners in a different fashion. But the fact is he chose to die on a cross. Although he did not point a gun at his own head and pull the trigger, he brought about, quite consciously and willfully, his own death.

If this is so, there can be, for the Christian, no general, legalistic condemnation of suicide. Each case must be judged on its own merits. Although suicide is often, perhaps usually, an expression of radical despair, it may also as self-sacrifice be an expression of profound faith and commitment. The basic question is not should I take my own life, but rather, for what purpose do I offer my life? The man who swallows poison in order to avoid giving testimony under torture which will lead to suffering on the part of innocent people may well be more righteous than the person who tells all in order to save his own skin.

## "YOU SHALL NOT COMMIT ADULTERY"

In a language as rich in sexual vocabulary as is Hebrew one might well expect to find many words denoting various shades and types of adultery. Such, however, is not the case. The word *na'ap*, which is employed in this seventh commandment, is used almost exclusively throughout the Old Testament to refer to the breaking of the marriage bond through sexual infidelity and to describe Israel's unfaithfulness to God. The breaking of the marriage bond through unfaithfulness is adultery, no matter what the circumstances.

Because adultery, unlike murder, is seldom committed unintentionally, little regard is paid in the Torah to the question of intention. One of the few exceptions to this rule reads as follows:

> If there is a betrothed virgin, and a man meets her in the city and lies with her, then you shall bring them both out to the gate of that city, and you shall stone them to death with stones, the young woman because she did not cry for help though she was in the city, and the man because he violated his neighbor's wife; so you shall purge the evil from the midst of you. But if in the open country a man meets a young woman who is betrothed, and the man seizes her and lies with her, then only the man who lay with her shall die. But to the young woman you shall do nothing (Deuteronomy 22:23–26).

Here at least is a modest consideration of intentionality, though one must admit that the law still seems extremely harsh from a modern vantage point. It is noteworthy that no such exception is made for a wife who is forced to commit adultery. Apparently, whether in the country or in the city she is subject to the death penalty, for she has, intentionally or not, broken the sacred bond of marriage.

Of course, in order to inflict the death penalty two witnesses are required. This, in itself, mitigates somewhat the stringency of the law, for if two witnesses are present, the possibility of rape is seriously reduced. Still, there might well be instances in which rape is consummated and yet the attacked wife is punished.

There are times, of course, when adultery is suspected, but no two witnesses can be found. Numbers 5 contains an account of how the jealous husband can test his wife's fidelity. She is to be taken to the priest who, after making the appropriate offering, administers to her "the water of bitterness," a concoction which is unspecified in content except that it is to contain dust from the floor of the Tabernacle. If the woman is innocent, it is said the water will cause no difficulty but will instead produce fertility. If, on the other hand, she is guilty, the waters will bring upon her a curse. Her belly will swell, her thigh will "fall away" and her guilt will be made plain. One wonders just how effective and accurate such a test really could be. One may well suspect that it was more effective as a deterrent than as a test. The wise woman, faced by such an ordeal, would at least do everything possible to allay her husband's suspicions.

In prohibiting adultery, the Decalogue of course promulgates a law which is commonly accepted throughout the world. Although the peoples of the earth differ considerably concerning the meaning and value of marriage, there are few who consider the act of adultery with indifference. The marital relation between man and woman is usually considered, if not a permanent relation, at least an important one which ought not to be destroyed by a third party. Like the sixth commandment, therefore, the seventh commandment finds many parallels in the law codes and customs of the *goi'im*. What is unique about Israel's attitude toward adultery is not to be found in the prohibition itself but in the positive attitude toward marriage which undergirds this defense of it.

## Marriage as Commitment

We have already discussed at some length the conception of marriage expressed in Scripture and there is no need to do more than review briefly what has already been said. In marriage *iš* and *iššah* unite as one flesh to reconstitute *'adam* and, in so doing, reflect the image of God. Male is meant for female and female, for male. Any attempt to hinder, pervert, or destroy this natural union is considered anathema, for marriage is an order blessed by God through creation. Furthermore, marriage in Israel is also meant to reflect the relation between God and his people consummated at Sinai. This covenant, which is a revelation of what the relation between man and woman is meant to be like, shows that marriage should be far more than simply a physical union between two persons, for the covenant demands ultimate commitment on the part of Israel and promises absolute faithfulness on the part of God. Just as Israel is commanded to love God with all her heart and soul and mind, so husband and wife are called to respond to each other with unqualified commitment. Only when such commitment is present does marriage truly reflect the divine covenant.

This is the hidden truth which Jesus makes plain in the Sermon on the Mount.

> "You have heard that it was said, 'You shall not commit adultery.'
> But I say to you that every one who looks at a woman lustfully
> has already committed adultery with her in his heart"
>
> (Matthew 5:27–28).

In saying this, Jesus is not propounding a new law but is rather pointing to the absolute demands inherent in Israel's long-standing conception of marriage. Because the male is meant to reflect the love of God for Israel, any thought, word or deed which expresses anything less than absolute faithfulness is a sign of sin. Adultery, therefore, cannot, in its deepest sense, be legalistically defined. Before God any act by the man or the woman which threatens the full unity of *'adam* is an act of adultery. Only in the light of this absolute commitment which marriage demands can the various questions concerning heterosexual relations be understood.

## Premarital Sexual Relations

For the Israelite, the meaning of sex is to be found in the act of commitment of two persons to each other. The act of sexual intercourse is the physical manifestation of the decision of the man and the woman to become one flesh, one *'adam*. When robbed of this dimension of personal commitment, sexuality is robbed of its inherent joy and meaning. The man or woman who thinks that pleasure can be separated from commitment attacks the very meaning of sex itself.

The commitment made between man and woman is formally expressed in the marriage ritual. Although we know little of the ceremony as it was ordered in early days, we can be reasonably sure that a covenant was made primarily between the two families involved and secondarily between the bride and groom. The groom committed himself by the paying of the *mohar* to the bride's father, and the bride's family committed her by accepting the contract of marriage. The marriage was then celebrated by a prolonged wedding feast in the house of the bridegroom which often lasted seven days.

The marriage, however, was essentially fulfilled and made final when male and female became one flesh through consummated sexual intercourse. In a sense, all of the commitments made in the marriage ceremony were only tokens and symbols of the real commitment made between the bride and groom in the sexual act. This belief that true marriage is to be found only in physical union underlies much of Israel's law concerning marriage.

It is undoubtedly for this reason that Deuteronomy says,

> If a man meets a virgin who is not betrothed, and seizes her and lies with her, and they are found, then the man who lay with her shall give to the father of the young woman fifty shekels of silver, and she shall be his wife, because he has violated her; he may not put her away all his days (Deuteronomy 22:28–29).

Thus the man who seduces or rapes a virgin is forced to confess openly what is already the case: through intercourse he has married her; she is his wife. The man who does not do this makes the girl an adulteress if she marries anyone else. Because they have become one flesh, she is his and he is hers.

This is also the reason why such care was taken to assure that a bride was indeed a virgin. The tokens of her virginity (the blood shed at the breaking of the maidenhead) were carefully preserved lest any question should later arise. Then, if the husband should ever charge that his wife was not a virgin when she married him, her father could produce these tokens (Deuteronomy

22:17–21). Virginity on the part of a woman was taken with extraordinary seriousness because of the view of marriage already discussed. If a bride had already had sexual relations with another man, she not only committed adultery on her wedding night herself; she also caused her husband to commit adultery as well. Thus an event which was meant to reflect God's image was radically perverted. An innocent man was led to perpetrate one of the most heinous of crimes, the murder of 'adam.

All of this means that for the Bible there is, in truth, no such thing as premarital sexual intercourse. Since sexual intercourse is, in fact, marriage, those who engage in such activities before being formally married are one flesh whether they know it or not. Formal marriage to anyone else, then, constitutes adultery. Conversely, if premarital sexual relations are followed by formal marriage, then Scripture offers no condemnation. In fact, it was customary for betrothed couples to live together before the marriage ceremony actually took place.[12]

What is important, then, is not that two persons be formally married in a religious ceremony but that they commit themselves to each other absolutely and without reservation. Persons who are formally married but who in fact make no such commitment are just as guilty, if not more so, than persons who engage in sexual relations without the benefit of an external ceremony. This is not to say that it is wise for couples to enter into sexual relations without the protection of a legal covenant, for to do so the couple must depend solely upon their own personal intentions to hold the marriage together. Nevertheless, their marriage is as much a marriage in the eyes of God as is that of any duly married couple.

## Birth Control

For many non-Roman Catholics the question of the use of contraceptives as a means of avoiding the conception of children

---

12. Mary and Joseph journeyed to Bethlehem together while only betrothed. Amusingly enough, in Medieval art they are sometimes pictured as traveling with a chaperon, apparently to remove any scandal attached to such premarital contact.

seems to be a purely pragmatic question. If one does not want more children, why not employ such artificial means to prevent pregnancy? The understanding of marriage as unqualified commitment, however, seems to raise questions about this prevalent view. If the essential meaning of marriage is to be found when male and female commit themselves unreservedly to become one flesh, does not the use of contraceptives undercut the true meaning of marriage? Does not the employment of the pill, the loop, and other such artificial devices mean that, in effect, man and woman are only "playing at" commitment? Does this not place an insurmountable barrier between man and woman so that they do not, in reality, become "one flesh"?

Those who argue this way supplement this argument with other references to Scripture.[13] They point out, for instance, that in Genesis 1 God commands man to be fruitful and multiply and in so doing provides one of the primary reasons for marriage. Moreover, they argue that since God is the giver of life, any use of contraceptives is an attempt to frustrate his will. Hence, the contraceptive is in fact a symbol of man's alienation from God and of sin.

Let us begin by examining the "supplementary" arguments first. It must be noted immediately that in Genesis God not only commands male and female to be fruitful and multiply; he also states the reasons for so doing. Man is to be fruitful in order that he may fill the earth and subdue it. In other words, the end of man is to dominate the earth; procreation is a means to that end. The fact is, however, that today man's fruitfulness is leading him not to dominion over creation but to subservience to his environment. Man has obeyed God all too well in this respect, for now there is a grave danger that, if our population continues to grow at anything like its present rate, the earth will soon no longer be able to support mankind. If man's chief end is to dominate the earth

13. Actually most Roman Catholics take the supplementary arguments to be the primary ones. The position of the Roman Catholic Church is based first and foremost upon natural law rather than upon an understanding of marriage as a covenantal commitment.

and subdue it, he must take care lest the means which God has provided lead him away from, rather than toward, this end.

The argument that because God is the giver of life the use of contraceptives must be avoided is specious, for it grasps only half of the paradox of free will and predestination. God does give life, but he works through man. Man's freedom is always involved in procreation, for every sexual act involves decision. Furthermore, man, in his efforts to dominate the earth, has already done much to root out disease and hence to lengthen man's life span. This is, in fact, one of the reasons why the population of the earth is increasing so rapidly. If one wishes to argue that man ought not to prevent pregnancies through the use of contraceptives then one ought to argue that "the Lord takes away" and that any use of medicine is an illegitimate frustration of God's will. Moreover, one should then also argue that the rhythm method of birth control and simple abstinence are attempts to frustrate God's will too.

The question still remains, however, whether the use of contraceptives denies the absolute commitment which man and woman are to offer each other in marriage. It must be said at the outset that if there is no desire at all to have children and if there is never intercourse without contraceptives, then the absolute commitment is broken. For marriage to reflect the image of God there must be a will to have children. It is also true, however, that both abstinence and continual procreation may be a threat to this bond of commitment. The refusal to use contraceptives may, in fact, express either the arrogance of the male who does not care how burdened his wife or his society is or the selfishness of the female who desires more children no matter what the cost. The man who enters the bonds of commitment with a woman must be concerned above all for her dignity and well-being; he must love her as God loves Israel. The wife, in turn, must also be concerned about the dignity and well-being of her husband, as Israel is concerned to love her God. Together, as 'adam, they are called to dominate the earth and use their creativity for the glory of God. If procreation helps in achieving this aim of mankind, then man should, indeed, be fruitful and multiply, but if it makes man a slave rather than a master then he shows his obedience to God by employing contraceptives. Marital commitment involves physical, but is always more than simply physical, commitment. In essence, the unqualified commitment of marriage is a manifestation of concern for the whole person and not just an agreement to produce as many children as possible.

## Monogamy

Thus far in this discussion of the seventh commandment it has generally been assumed that marriage is a monogamous relation between one man and one woman. As even the casual student of the Bible knows, however, polygamy, if not polyandry, was widely practiced in ancient Israel. Furthermore, in the New Testament there is no specific prohibition of polygamy either. To be sure, in 1 Timothy 3:2 it is said that a bishop of the church should have only one wife, but this seems to imply rather than deny that polygamy was practiced by early Christians, for it makes monogamy a special qualification for bishops. If this is the case, what attitude should modern Christians take toward the question of monogamy?

Although Israelites did practice polygamy, it must also be recognized that her basic myth of marriage, found in Genesis 2–3, seems to regard monogamy as the "natural" state of man. The statement, "therefore a man leaves his father and his mother and cleaves to his wife, and they become one flesh," might be regarded as consistent with polyandry but certainly not with polygamy, for here the emphasis is upon the faithfulness of a man to his wife. The fact that only one woman was taken from 'adam further underlines this point.

The idea of the covenant as a prototype for human marital relations also sheds light upon the biblical view of marriage, for this "archetypal pattern" surely denies polyandry. Just as Israel can have only one husband, so wives must do the same. The Old Covenant, however, does not specifically preclude polygamy, for nowhere does Yahweh promise to love only Israel. Israel is bound, but her husband is free to take other brides if he so wills. The New Covenant, on the other hand, seems to deny this justification for polygamy, for in Christ the covenant is opened to all men. Hence, it would seem that only one marriage is possible for God and for his reflection, the human husband.

Still, it must be recognized that Scripture makes no absolute statements in this regard. Early followers of Jesus, at least, believed that they were free to have more than one wife as long as those wives could be supported responsibly. Thus it would appear that Christians are freed from any binding law of monogamy. I do not mean to say that the laws concerning bigamy in, say, the United States should forthwith be abandoned. These laws doubtless express the basic convictions of the American people concerning marriage and surely serve a useful purpose. Nevertheless, it must be recognized that bigamy is simply a crime against the state; there are no firm biblical grounds for saying that it is also a sin against God. In countries where polygamy is found, the Christian church is free to allow the practice if it seems useful to do so.[14] It might also be argued that in a country in which a large segment of the male population has been killed in a war, polygamy might be countenanced. For the Bible, at least, it is far more important for every person who is physically able to enter the bonds of marriage than that the marriage be monogamous. In a situation where the number of males is roughly equivalent to the number of females, therefore, monogamy should be supported lest some be deprived of the marital relationship.

## Perversion

Because Scripture emphasizes the supreme importance and value of heterosexual relations, it also condemns all sorts of

14. It is interesting that at the present time this is a matter of great urgency for missionaries in certain African countries. In lands where polygamy is the norm, the insistence of the church that monogamy be practiced constitutes an attack upon the very basis of society and subjects the convert to very difficult problems.

"abnormal" sexual activity which in any way might preclude or pervert the true unity of *'adam.* In particular, incest,[15] homosexuality,[16] and bestiality[17] are regarded as anathema, for each of these perversions prevents the true unity of *'adam.* Each is, in its own way, a form of adultery.

Although today the original reasons for these laws are often forgotten and the penalties prescribed softened, the basic biblical aversion to the perversion of normal heterosexual relations still dominates our culture. In fact, no one group in modern America is so ostracized or condemned out-of-hand as is the sexually perverted "caste." As Pierre Berton says, homosexuals are to modern culture what lepers were to the ancient world.[18]

This comparison of homosexuals to lepers, of course, raises an important question for the church. Should not the church today seek to minister to these outcasts in the same way that Jesus and his followers sought to minister to the lepers? Has the church been justified in her silent but effective ostracization of the sexually abnormal? Should she not reach out to these outcasts, not to condemn but to cure?

In the light of what has already been said, it is clear that the church if true to her theological heritage must affirm the value of heterosexual relations. At the same time, the people of God are in the world not to condemn but to heal. Therefore, the faithful must repond with compassion and understanding to those who exhibit these marks of sin. It is not enough passively to offer forgiveness of sins to men in general. If the church is to be true to her Master, she must seek out the lost and offer, where possible, help and even reassurance.

This, of course, will be an unpopular ministry, for there are many both within and without the church who fear infectious

15. Leviticus 18:6–18; Deuteronomy 27:20, 22.
16. Leviticus 18:22.
17. Leviticus 18:23; Deuteronomy 27:21.
18. Pierre Berton, *The Comfortable Pew* (New York: J. B. Lippincott Co., 1965), p. 78.

contact with these outcasts.[19] It will take courage to appeal directly to these modern "lepers" and to encourage the state to take a more enlightened attitude toward them. If the church believes, however, that the covenant does mediate the power of reconciliation, then this is a task which cannot be avoided. Perhaps the best way for the church to begin this ministry is by accenting rather than rejecting the joys of normal heterosexual relations. If the church is to be true to her biblical heritage, she must cast off the aura of prudish Victorianism and learn once more the truth so beautifully conveyed in the Song of Songs. Only then will she be able to minister to others who reject this truth.

## *Divorce*

In the light of Israel's emphasis upon the value of marriage and the ultimate commitment which it entails, it may seem strange that little is said in the Torah about the subject of divorce. Some passages, of which a few have already been cited, indicate those situations in which a divorce may not take place, but only in Deuteronomy do we find any discussion of the proper grounds for divorce. Even here much is left unsaid.

> When a man takes a wife and marries her, if then she finds no favor in his eyes because he has found some indecency in her, and he writes her a bill of divorce and puts it in her hand and sends her out of his house, and she departs out of his house, and if she goes and becomes another man's wife, and the latter husband dislikes her and writes her a bill of divorce and puts it in her hand and sends her out of his house, or if the latter husband dies, who took her to be his wife, then her former husband, who sent her away, may not take her again to be his wife, after she has been defiled; for that is an abomination before the LORD, and you shall not bring guilt upon the land which the LORD your God gives you for an inheritance (Deuteronomy 24:1–4).

The word translated here "indecency" is in Hebrew *'erwah,* and means more literally "nakedness or shame." Although "indecency"

19. Ibid., p. 79.

196

or, as the new Jewish translation of the Torah would have it, "obnoxiousness," conveys something of the meaning of *'erwah*, neither captures its full, but ambiguous meaning. Probably, this word refers to any one of a number of repugnant characteristics which might offend the husband. The vagueness of the term seems to suggest that the husband was free to divorce his wife for any reason which he himself found sufficient.

There have been during the history Israel, many who have rejected such a loose interpretation of the passage. The famous first century rabbi, Shammai, for instance, argued that adultery is the only legitimate ground for divorce and waged a battle of interpretation against all those who thought otherwise. Apparently, he did not stand with the majority of Jews, for the divorce law during the time of Jesus was very liberal and divorce was a common occurrence.

Although Jesus seems in some instances[20] to side with Shammai, he actually goes much further.

> And Pharisees came up and in order to test him asked, "Is it lawful for a man to divorce his wife?" He answered them, "What did Moses command you?" They said, "Moses allowed a man to write a certificate of divorce, and to put her away." But Jesus said to them, "For your hardness of heart he wrote you this commandment. But from the beginning of creation, 'God made them male and female.' 'For this reason a man shall leave his father and mother and be joined to his wife, and the two shall become one.' So they are no longer two but one. What therefore God has joined together, let not man put asunder" (Mark 10:2–9).

In saying this Jesus returns to the conception of marriage as a relation of absolute commitment already discussed. In marriage, male and female can no longer think of themselves as two persons but only as one *'adam*. Any breaking of this commitment and this union is a sin against God. Ideally, there should be no divorce. No man or woman can divorce his or her spouse and think that nothing wrong has happened in the eyes of God.

20. Matthew 19:9.

Jesus, then, carries the biblical position in regard to marriage as it is sketched out in Genesis 1 to its logical, if radical, conclusion. At the same time, it must be recognized that Jesus is making clear the ultimate demands of the covenant, not setting forth a piece of civil legislation. The fact is that hardness of heart remains and men and women are not perfected. Hence, both civil and ecclesiastical law must take sin into account when establishing rules of conduct for a given community. Jesus' teachings about divorce should no more be legalized than should his commandment, "You, therefore, must be perfect, as your heavenly Father is perfect" (Matthew 5:48).

This does not mean, of course, that the state ought to allow divorce for just any reason. Civil government has a duty to require reasonable grounds for divorce, lest the institution of marriage be governed by the tyranny of whim. To think that a modern, secular state should be ordered according to some saying of Jesus torn out of its proper context, however, is sheer folly. A civil law which denies all divorces except for reasons of adultery represents a bad misreading of the gospel and can only lead to hypocrisy, evasion, and personal tragedy.

The church must affirm with Jesus the belief that divorce is an evil which reflects man's hardness of heart. The church must also recognize, however, that because sin remains, divorce may well be the lesser of two evils in a given situation. An unhappy marriage may be a greater evil for the man and woman and their children than is a divorce. The lives of children can be irreparably damaged by friction between loveless parents. It is the duty of the church to seek the reconciliation of man and woman wherever possible, but it is also the duty of the church to protect the well-being of the individual too. Holy Communion should be available, not just to the righteous (if there are any), but to the truly repentant.

Furthermore, when a divorce occurs, the church should abandon all talk about guilty and innocent parties. In the first place, the breaking of an absolute commitment involves guilt no matter what the circumstances. Second, within the bond of marriage, two have become one. As such, they share the guilt of each other. Third, before the absolute demands of God's covenant there is no such thing as real innocence, for no man can live up to the call of God. Jesus comes to make clear what the radical demands of God are by showing us how man was and is meant to live, but he also comes to grant forgiveness to those who truly repent and acknowledge their hardness of heart.

## The New Morality

Many people, both inside and outside the church are much concerned these days that the traditional sexual ethics of Christendom are under severe attack. The automobile, the pill, and the general breakdown of parental authority have all led to an anything-goes attitude toward sex. Premarital and extramarital sexual relations are common. So are relations, which by the standards of previous generations, were called perversions. The question is: What attitude should the believer take toward this "new morality" which is so lauded by some and so attacked by others? Is he bound to attack or can he find some good in this moral revolution?

Before answering these questions it must be observed that the believer ought not to be unduly surprised by what has taken place. The biblical attitude toward sex is not based just upon a natural law which is recognized by all men but grows out of a response of faith to the covenant. Although the seventh commandment itself is paralleled in many pagan codes of law, it is itself based upon a positive meaning found in God's covenantal relation to his people. What once appeared, however, as a joyful virtue now appears as a repressive taboo. The sexual revolution is not so much the result of modern technology and freedom as it is a reflection of our culture's general reversion to paganism.

Still, the new morality calls the church to take a good hard look at the biblical tradition and to ask what aspects of it must be preserved as essential. Harvey Cox, in *The Secular City,* has attempted to do just this. In a chapter entitled "Sex and Secularity" he analyzes the sexual myths and mores of modern American culture and seeks to develop a Christian approach to the whole problem. Most people, I think, will find his opening attack upon the cult of "the Girl" and "the Playboy" both amusing and persuasive, but when he turns his attack upon the church and its "town ethic," many will be less amused.

Too much effort, Cox says, has been spent by Christians defending town mores and, in particular, a very artificially defined line of virginity which, as a matter of fact, retards rather than encourages sexual maturity. The church, he says, has been guilty of a dreadful hypocrisy which has only produced confusion and guilt feelings on the part of its members.

> Perhaps one day we in America will put away childish things and become mature men and women who do not have to rely on male and female deities of the mass media to tell us what to be. Perhaps one day we will outgrow our ridiculous obsession with sex, of which our fixation on chastity and virginity is just the other side of the coin. Until that time, however, we should rejoice that in Jesus Christ we are freed from myth and from Law. We are placed in a community of selves, free to the extent that we live for each other, free to develop whatever styles of life will contribute to the maturation of persons in a society where persons are often overlooked as we scamper to pursue profits and piety all at once.[21]

Cox's criticism of both American culture and the church is, in part, well taken. Surely hypocritical standards and a large amount of double thinking are involved in contemporary sexual ethics. It is also true, however, that the church has often spoken far more maturely and constructively than he gives her credit. Furthermore, when he begins to speak in a constructive vein one wonders just how well he understands the meaning of Christian freedom.

21. Harvey Cox, *The Secular City: Secularization and Urbanization in Theological Perspective* (New York: Macmillan Co., 1965), p. 216. Used by permission.

As I have tried to argue throughout this volume, the Torah, when rightly conceived, is not opposed to, but is an expression of, freedom. The Decalogue is the structure in which freedom can develop. The Law only becomes a harsh and unremitting legalism when the basic impulse of the Law, that is, the word which God speaks, is no longer heard. This is what has happened to many in the twentieth century. Because God's word is not heard, biblical norms are turned into a new kind of legalism. The positive virtue of chastity becomes a very legalized and artificial line of virginity. Cox is quite right in appealing to the New Testament as an antidote for such moralizing.

When the New Testament speaks of freedom from the law, however, it does not mean freedom from all norms of human behavior. Paul, for example, asserts that when one hears God's word spoken in Jesus Christ, what was once mere legalism now takes on a richer and fuller meaning. The hearer no longer need worry about the minute prescriptions and proscriptions of the Torah, for the word gives the essential impulse and meaning of life. Virginity is no longer just a negative limit but a positive virtue in which one can take joy. The seventh commandment is no longer an oppressive prohibition with "loopholes," but a positive reminder of our responsibility to foster and encourage the marriage relationship.

What Cox really does is to give up one law and myth so that he can accept the law and myth of maturation. I am not at all sure that this myth without any clarification is a better guide for conduct than is the mythology of *Playboy* magazine. It may provide only a tyranny of vagueness whereby the individual is left not with freedom but with confusion and misunderstanding. How does one, after all, distinguish between the mature and the immature, an obsession with sex and a genuine concern for an important aspect of existence, the natural and the perverted? How can one live "for another" without some mutually accepted patterns of life and norms for behavior? It is all well and good to say that we must live for one another, but unless we agree about the nature and destiny of *'adam,* such living for one another may end in pure chaos. Man must have myths which provide the structures by which to live. The choice is not between myth and no myth, for man cannot live without myths. The choice is for or against the myth of *'adam.*

The "virtue" of virginity conceived of as a "line" which must not be crossed may, indeed, produce hypocrisy and immaturity and undoubtedly needs to be challenged, but this does not mean that the virtue of chastity should be discarded. On the contrary, those who wish to live for others must recognize that living for others demands the making of commitments which cannot be broken. Becoming one flesh with another is such a commitment and it is precisely in this commitment that the joy and meaning of sex is found. An attack upon chastity as a virtue is, in fact, an attack upon the meaning of sex. Covertly, it is an attack upon the permanence of the covenant of God with Israel as well.

### "YOU SHALL NOT STEAL"

Like the prohibitions of murder and adultery, the prohibition of stealing is not unique to Israel but finds many parallels in pagan codes of law. What is distinctive about the eighth commandment is not found in what it says but in the word upon which it is based. The prohibition of stealing, for Israel, flows out of several positive motifs already emphasized in this and preceding chapters. In particular, stealing is forbidden because it is (1) an attack upon the dignity of man and his work, (2) a refusal to accept and rejoice in what God has given, (3) an attack upon the reconciliation of man and the land. In a word, stealing is an attack upon the covenant and its fruits.

### *Kidnapping and Slavery*

The most vicious form of stealing is, undoubtedly, kidnapping. Since the institution of slavery was widespread throughout the ancient Near East, this type of stealing was more common than it is today, for a kidnapped person could readily be sold for a profit. The Covenant Code makes plain the seriousness of such an offense. "Whoever steals a man, whether he sells him or is found in possesion of him, shall be put to death" (Exodus 21:16). A man's freedom is God-given and therefore should not be taken from him by stealth. Kidnapping is in direct violation of the meaning of the covenant.

There were, to be sure, Hebrews who were either sold into slavery by their parents or who, for one reason or another, sold themselves as slaves. In these instances, the Torah limits the duration of enslavement, thus mitigating somewhat this attack upon human dignity (Exodus 21:2–3). In Exodus 21:7–11, special provisions are also made for a daughter sold into slavery. Thus, slavery, as an institution, is accepted, but safeguards are provided, lest the dignity of an Israelite be destroyed by it.

## The Stealing of Goods and Other Property

According to the Bible one of the ways in which man both reflects and obeys God is by working. Labor, particularly creative labor, is not something to escape but an activity to engage in joyfully, for in work God's image is made manifest. It is right and just, then, that that which a man creates or obtains through his work is his to use and dispose of responsibly. The thief attacks a part of man's dignity both by taking the fruits of someone else's labor and by refusing to reflect God in honest work himself.

Thus any attempt to gain goods, property, or money without honest labor is condemned by law. Not only is stealing forbidden, the use of false weights is condemned in both the Deuteronomic Code (Deuteronomy 25:13–16) and in Leviticus 19:35. The Covenant Code also includes provisions dealing with breaches of trust (Exodus 22:9), the leaving of a dangerous open pit (Exodus 21:33), and the misuse of fire (Exodus 22:6). In fact, this early Code goes far beyond the negative command not to steal by implying throughout that each Israelite is responsible for the preservation and well-being of the property of his neighbor (Exodus 23:4–5).

Leviticus contains the following expansion of the eighth commandment.

> You shall not steal, nor deal falsely, nor lie to one another. And you shall not swear by my name falsely, and so profane the name of your God; I am the LORD (Leviticus 19:11).

Thus the commandment is seen to exclude any act of deceit or treachery and to foster an attitude of esteem for both the dignity of others and one's own integrity. The Israelite here is reminded that since he exists "in the name of Yahweh" there are no loopholes in the law. Stealing is stealing whether it be executed through an act of stealth or as a word of deceit to a customer.

## The Right to Own Private Property

Thus far we have discussed the actions involving the property of others which are forbidden by law. A very pressing ideological question remains to be discussed: Is property necessary? Is Campbell Morgan correct when he asserts: Broadly speaking, the eighth commandment forbids all forms of communism which deny man's right to property.[22] Should the eighth commandment be taken, as it often is, to be a biblical basis for the modern, Western belief in the "sanctity of private property"?

In answering this question it must first be recognized that the Bible does not emphasize at any time the "rights of man." The Israelite possesses property through the grace of God, but not because he has a natural right to it. This is made particularly clear in connection with Israel's possession of the land. In Leviticus God is quoted as saying,

> The land shall not be sold in perpetuity, for the land is mine; for you are strangers and sojourners with me. And in all the country you possess, you shall grant a redemption of the land
> (Leviticus 25:23–24).

22. Morgan, *The Ten Commandments,* pp. 92–93.

Thus Israel has no property rights at all, for she maintains her relation to the land only through the grace of God. When her disobedience becomes too great, God takes the land from her and sends her into exile.

Nevertheless, the Christian must be critical of any philosophy or political party which finds the root of evil in property ownership. Although human sin may be exhibited as an acquisitive desire for material security, there is no reason to think that the removal of property will remove all social evils. The history of Communism in the twentieth century has shown quite conclusively that the abolition of private property does not constitute the removal of all social evil. Moreover, recent developments in Communist countries indicate that private property and the profit motive are far more difficult to abolish than some nineteenth century visionaries thought. There seems to be a natural human tendency to want to own goods and property which cannot be quickly, if ever, erased. Thus, as a practical social system, pure Communism is difficult to implement, for it seems to go against the grain of man.

The fact that Communism falls short of its stated ideals, however, should not lead to smugness or complacency on the part of the capitalistic West. With its emphasis upon man's acquisitiveness, capitalism has often led to terrible abuses. In the name of the profit motive and with the slogan that "business is business" all kinds of inhumanity to man have not only been tolerated but justified. To be sure, social legislation in the twentieth century has vanquished some of the worst excesses, but this does not mean that the evils of capitalism have been destroyed.

Somehow we have developed a society in which everyone has so much that no one is satisfied. While affluence reigns, the land suffers from the ravages of tedium and no one seems able to change it. Appeals to sex as a way of selling detergents, garish neon-lit stands cluttering our roadsides, and endless recitals about the glories and hopes for a Great Society seem meaningless and yet inevitable. Before we condemn an alternative social system such as Communism for its difficulties we ought first to look much more critically at our own.

## "YOU SHALL NOT BEAR FALSE WITNESS"

Although this ninth commandment is often taken to be equivalent to a prohibition of lying in general, its original meaning was doubtless much more restricted in scope. Literally the Hebrew means: "You shall not respond with deceitful testimony against your fellow citizen." Although *rēʻ* may mean friend, companion, or neighbor, it is probably best translated fellow citizen. The "your" emphasizes the bond which exists among citizens. Whether friend or foe, the fellow citizen is not just "a" person; he is "your" person. Therefore, since this bond of citizenship does exist, the Israelite ought not to testify falsely in a court of law.

It is significant that the one commandment of the Decalogue which speaks at all directly about citizenship refers to responsibility in the court of justice rather than responsibility to the king. To be sure, the mention of a king in the book of Exodus would be anachronistic, but had Israel conceived of the claims of the royal leader as absolute and all-important she could have included such a commandment as "You shall not disobey the human ruler of Israel." The fact that she did not do so—the king is alluded to only a few times in the whole Torah—shows that the kings never were accorded the power and authority so common in other lands in the ancient Near East.[23] The sons of David some-

---

23. There may well be some who will protest this minimizing of the importance of the king for the life and religion of Israel. In recent years, a number of important scholars have sought to show that the development of the kingship produced vast changes in the religion of Israel and led to a view of the king similar to that held in many other, particularly Mesopotamian countries. It is true, of course, that with David and Solomon the kingship did become extremely important. Israel's Temple was first and foremost the king's chapel. Many of the Psalms (see, for instance, Psalms 2, 82, 93, and 97) reflect a somewhat new attitude toward the kingship of both man and God. Nevertheless, the books of Samuel and Kings also reveal a very honest and critical attitude toward human royal authority. Solomon may be described as a son of God but he also is depicted as a somewhat ruthless ruler who brought oppression to Israel. Throughout the Old Testament a very candid and critical attitude toward human authority seems to prevail.

times ruled with a heavy hand, but in principle, at least, they themselves were subject to the law. Justice was meted out not through royal whim, but according to the will of Yahweh.

Unfortunately, we do not know precisely how the courts of law operated during Israel's long history or exactly what status the law, as we now know it in the Torah, had. Occasionally the Torah and the historical writings give us glimpses of Israelite justice in operation,[24] but it is very difficult to ascertain how widespread the practices described really were. Most important, it is not at all clear just when and how the legal prescriptions and proscriptions of the law came into existence. Were these laws in use for centuries in preexilic Israel or were they largely the expression of postexilic Judaism? If they were in existence before the fall of Jerusalem, were they used throughout Israel as a basis for court decisions or were they only precedents developed by individual judges and courts for use in their communities? Many calculated guesses have been made about these questions and there is no need to review them here. Perhaps all that needs to be said is that it is now clear that although the Torah did not take final shape until the postexilic period, many, if not most, of the laws were in existence and in effect in preexilic Israel.

Whatever the precise status of a given law in a given period was, one fact is certain: the whole judicial system rested upon the testimony of witnesses. In Deuteronomy, for instance, it is stated:

> A single witness shall not prevail against a man for any crime or for any wrong in connection with any offence that he has committed; only on the evidence of two witnesses, or of three witnesses, shall a charge be sustained (Deuteronomy 19:15).

Because justice in Israel depended so much upon witnesses, it is quite understandable that the ninth commandment is included among the ten. It is, indeed, the cornerstone of civil law and jus-

24. There are several examples of jurisprudence in action in Israel. For one example, see 1 Kings 21:8–14.

tice. As long as Israelites felt compelled to speak the truth in court, justice could be maintained. The bearing of false witness was not only an attack upon another individual, it was an undermining of the whole structure of civil justice.

There were, of course, procedures developed by which the court might test the witnesses. In fact, one of the main tasks of the judges was the examining and cross-examining of the witnesses. Accusing witnesses were questioned separately by the judges and their testimony compared. Only when two witnesses agreed in detail could punishment be imposed upon the accused. Deuteronomy outlines the punishment for a false witness:

> If a malicious witness rises against any man to accuse him of wrongdoing, then both parties to the dispute shall appear before the LORD, before the priests and the judges who are in office in those days; the judges shall inquire diligently, and if the witness is a false witness and has accused his brother falsely, then you shall do to him as he had meant to do to his brother; so you shall purge the evil from the midst of you
>
> (Deuteronomy 19:16–20).

Although this method may not have been foolproof, it must have acted as a deterrant to the man who wished to damage the reputation or inflict unwarranted punishment upon a fellow citizen. Its weakness, however, is illustrated by the ease with which Naboth was unjustly convicted (1 Kings 21:13) when two base fellows were "planted" as witnesses.

Although justice is severely threatened by the lies of false witnesses, it is also imperiled by the silence of those who know the truth. Hence Leviticus includes the following admonition:

> If any one sins in that he hears a public adjuration to testify and though he is a witness, whether he has seen or come to know the matter, yet does not speak, he shall bear his iniquity
>
> (Leviticus 5:1).

Whether any penalty was imposed by the court for such silence is not clear. Probably, it was thought that God himself would punish the man who failed to bring justice to pass by his lack of testimony. The idea that silence may also be a form of bearing false witness is, at any rate, one concerning which modern men might well be reminded. Not only the liar who commits perjury but the silent witness who vanishes into the crowd impedes justice in this world and stands condemned before God.

Thus far we have dealt with the ninth commandment as referring specifically to telling the truth in a court of law. Although such a restriction of the commandment is quite justified and proper, the spirit of the Decalogue, with its emphasis upon the value and dignity of man, impels the reader to see also a broader meaning. If one begins with the recognition that all men have worth, this commandment can then be legitimately interpreted as meaning, "Always speak the truth about your neighbor." There should be no slander (Leviticus 19:16), no false reporting (Exodus 23:1), no unwarranted attack upon a person's or a family's good name (Deuteronomy 22:18).

For the Bible, a man's name is his most sacred possession, for it is the vocalization of his very self, his reality in the society of men. Therefore, although there is little concern expressed in Scripture regarding little fibs and white lies, great emphasis is placed upon the importance of basic honesty and integrity when dealing with others. Israel is (or should be) bound together by 'emet, truth, for God's name is truth itself.

"YOU SHALL NOT COVET YOUR NEIGHBOR'S HOUSE; YOU SHALL NOT COVET YOUR NEIGHBOR'S WIFE, OR HIS MAN-SERVANT, OR HIS MAIDSERVANT, OR HIS OX, OR HIS ASS, OR ANYTHING THAT IS YOUR NEIGHBOR'S"

Just as all of the commandments flow naturally out of the preamble to the Decalogue and depend upon it, so also do they flow toward the tenth "word," for the last commandment is an expression of the inner spirit which informs all the others. This is the "word" which plugs all loopholes, closes all gaps, and reveals with startling clarity how demanding God's word to Israel really is.

All of the other commandments can be and have been interpreted as simply requiring or prohibiting some outward action.[25]

25. As has been argued, of course, obedience to the commandments, when correctly understood, does involve inward intention as well as outward action.

God's final word to Israel in the Decalogue, however, reveals that true obedience involves not only a change in action but a complete transformation of intention as well. There have been, to be sure, exegetes who have argued that even the tenth commandment concerns primarily outward action. This interpretation rests upon the assumption that the word *hamad,* which is here translated covet, means to desire with the intent to take. That is to say, covetousness only becomes such when it issues in outward action.

Such an interpretation, however, can be demonstrated to be false on two grounds. First of all, if the tenth commandment prohibits only the outward manifestations of inordinate and selfish desire then it is superfluous, since the preceding commandments have already dealt with such actions. Second, the Deuteronomic Decalogue supplements the one in Exodus by adding a prohibition of *'awah,* that is, desire for or longing after someone else's property. This may be simply an example of Hebraic parallelism, but it also makes clear that the commandment deals with intention and not just action.

The tenth commandment, then, prohibits the inordinate desire of any one or any thing belonging to someone else. The question of what exactly an "inordinate" desire is, however, is a difficult one. Surely, the prohibition does not mean that an Israelite ought not to want what he does not have. Rather, the intent of the commandment seems to be to prohibit any envy, jealousy, or greed.

Israel has been given an inheritance, a land flowing with milk and honey. Each Israelite has been given abilities and powers as God has seen fit. And God has commanded that every person use these abilities by working for six days. An Israelite can work hard and hope, quite legitimately, for a good return for his labor. He need not feel at all ashamed in wanting a day's wages for a day's work; that is not covetousness. But when the Israelite has used his talents and has received his share, he must not be jealous of what his neighbor has. He must put away dissatisfaction with his portion, for his portion is given by God.

There is little emphasis anywhere in the Bible upon the kind of negative fatalism so characteristic of, say, Islam. The Israelite knew himself to be a free man who can use his wits and his talents to survive. Poverty, disease, and human degradation are not meant to be accepted with a shrug of the shoulders as the will of God. Yahweh is the God who rescues and frees, not the God who grinds the poor into the dust. Nevertheless, the Israelite, at his best at least, knew the secret of contentment. Envy and jealousy have no bounds; their fruit is discontent and finally crime. If covetousness were absent, it is doubtful that murder, adultery, stealing, or bearing false witness would ever occur. The New Testament has it that the love of money is the root of all evils (1 Timothy 6:10); the Old puts it more exactly: covetousness in all its forms is the basic source of social disorder.

Nowhere in the rest of the Torah is this commandment concerning covetousness further elaborated. This, of course, is hardly surprising. One could no more enforce a general law against covetousness than one could enforce a law against obscene thoughts. The law, as a legal code, can only deal with actions, not unexpressed intentions. Thus the tenth commandment shows, as do the others when understood correctly, that finally the Decalogue is not a set of legal rules and regulations at all. Rather, it is a word of grace spoken to Israel. When God's voice is heard, the Decalogue can be understood as the structure of freedom. Through it the God of freedom is glorified and the dignity of man preserved.

When a people hears, understands, and "lives" the tenth commandment, that people knows true freedom. Political and economic tyranny enslave men, to be sure, but there is no more insidious form of tyranny than that of covetousness. A man who covets can know no peace, no *šalom*. His reconciliation with his fellow men and with God is shattered, for he has lost the secret of contentment. Nothing can satisfy him, for greed knows no bounds. The tenth commandment, then, reveals to us the inner secret of human freedom. Freedom is not so much doing what one likes as it is liking what one does.

# INDEX

# KEY WORDS

215

## SOURCES AND AUTHORS

## PROPER NAMES

# Index

## HEBREW AND GREEK WORDS AND LATIN PHRASES

## BIBLICAL REFERENCES